Sparklers

High Scoring Test Essays

and What They Teach Us

Gretchen Bernabei and Judy Reimer

Trail of Breadcrumbs

San Antonio, Texas

Trail of Breadcrumbs

www.trailofbreadcrumbs.net

ISBN: 978-0-9740629-1-4

Front cover by Johnny Ponce

Manufactured in San Antonio, Texas, in the United States of America on acid-free paper

For Nancy Considine

whose graceful work illuminates the writing

of teachers and students

all over Texas

Acknowledgments

Thank you to all of the students and parents who allowed us to share these wonderful pieces of writing.

We also wish to express our gratitude and admiration to the following people, for their enthusiastic assistance with this project:

Kim Grauer, Barry Lane, Jayne Hover, Dottie Hall, Jenny Guerrero, Patricia S. Gray, Betsty Kiker, Pat Feola, Sue Shoopman King, Jamie "I've Got Her Phone Number Memorized" Feola.

Thank you to the following school people whose cooperation has been invaluable:

Debbie Neeley, Killeen ISD; Denise Smith, Lubbock ISD; Joanna Minardi, Leander ISD; Cordell Jones, Alamo Heights ISD; Jenny Wilde and Pam Abbott in San Angelo ISD; Gail Clark in Teague ISD; Cynthia Candler and Mike Melugin, from Terrell ISD; Carol Bradshaw, Midland ISD, Cynthia Piña and Julie Schweers, Tom Davern, David Braddam, Lisa Braddam, Barbara Edens, Jana Laven, Roberta Schultze, Harry Stone and Cathy McFeaters, Northside ISD; Amy Stengel from North East ISD.

Thank you to John Negrete from Matson Multi Media and Simon Esparza and his colleagues from Cenveo San Antonio.

And a special thank you to Sandra Poth, Northside ISD.

Finally, thank you to our families and our wonderful husbands.

Introduction

We know that nothing teaches us about writing test scores more reliably than live student papers that have scored high.

We know that compositional risks encourage other compositional risks.

We know that sharing our information about what works makes us all stronger and smarter.

But probably most importantly, we know that students learn faster from each other than they learn from us.

We think the papers in this collection speak for themselves, but while putting this group of papers together, we made a few decisions we'd like to explain.

- We cleaned up a little spelling. Putting ourselves into the shoes of the writers, we cleaned up only those parts which might be embarrassing, those which the writers would probably have changed with a second look. We intentionally left in some of the spelling errors that demonstrate risk, in which the students "took a shot" at spelling a word they might not have known.

- We left mistakes in punctuation right where they occurred, for the most part. For a couple of writing teachers, it was difficult not to fix apostrophes here and there, so we have been sitting on our hands for a little while now. It's informative to see that papers can be imperfect and still earn the highest scores.

- We don't necessarily know which ones are fiction. Some clearly are, and some might be. That's a wonderful topic for classroom discussion. But if any of the content disturbs you deeply, write us and we'll fill you in on what we know about that piece.

- We did not write the prompts that went with each paper. Nor did we list the years the papers were written. We remembered signing confidentiality oaths every year we administered any tests, and it felt like we didn't have the right to publish the prompts. We don't think it matters, though. It's clear to see that all of the papers are produced from prompts about meaningful thoughts or moments in the students' lives, with permission to translate that meaning into any form or genre (besides poetry) which people have devised, including combinations of genres. And if anyone wants to see prompts from released tests, they're available on the web site of the Texas Education Agency. (Or put together into a list found on www.trailofbreadcrumbs.net.)

- We wrote craft lessons on some, but not on all, of the papers. If we'd taken another year to work on this project, we could have written several craft lessons for each paper, since each writer employed so many different kinds of approaches and techniques.

- We wrote "high school" instead of "grade 10" or "grade 11" or "grade 12" for the high school pieces. Travis Moncus is the only student whose grade is listed, and that's because we used two of his pieces, one from his 10th grade year and one from his 11th grade year.

We hope that you enjoy reading these pieces as much as we did, and that you find amusement and amazement in the many flashes of brilliance in the coming pages. With those ideas in mind, we are honored to offer this collection of papers from all across Texas.

Gretchen Bernabei and Judy Reimer

Table of Contents

Grade 4 Essays

Grade 7 Essays

Grade 7 Essays, continued

High School Essays

Grade 4 Essays with Craft Lessons

Grade 7 Essays with Craft Lessons

High School Essays with Craft Lessons

Appendix

Essays

Ha-choo! Ha-choo! Wow, Trey you have a huge cold. Well, I got your ham and cheese you asked for. "Thanks Ross," he said. Today my little brother, Trey, is very sick with a temperature of 101.2 so, I have to serve him. "Trey would you like anything else?" I asked. "No thank you." "I'll be in the living room watching TV. I said. While I was watching TV I was really wondering how long I was going to serve him because if I serve him to long he might start treating me like his slave.

When my TV show was over I went back into my brother's and I's room to see how Trey was doing. As I went into the room, I saw that he was playing a video game and he wasn't screaming for anything. So I asked mom if I could take Trey's temperature and she said it was o.k. I zoomed to Trey and took his temperature, he was 99.5. "Trey, guest what!" I yelled. "What" he screamed. "You are only 99.5, that means you're getting better!"

That night Trey had a pretty stuffed up nose, tissue after tissue. By the time his nose wasn't stuffed up anymore he asked very nicely if could have a chocolate. I was very surprised. After he ate his chocolate I took his temperature. He was 98.6! "Trey you're 98.6, you're better"! "Yes! I'm not sick anymore!" he yelled with joy. "Maybe I was wrong, just because you help someone doesn't mean they are going to treat you like a slave. What was I thinking.

Have you ever helped someone because he was your best friend? Well I have…and I never will again.

My friend Mark took me by the hand and dragged me to the school's wall. He popped his bright pink bubble gum bubble in my face. "Listen" he said. "I have a football game in Denver tomorrow, and I can't miss it." "Okay" I said, "What about it?" "Can you watch Rex?" he asked. Now I've watched his ant farm, his pet taranchula, and even his mouse. But Rex…NO WAY! I was not going to watch the dog who ripped my pants, ate my 50,000 dollar retainer, and bites me every week. "Come on," he said. "I'll take you to the Beatles concert." "Okay" I said, being a little hesitant. "Tomorrow morning at 8:00." "Got it" I said. When I got to his house the next morning, I saw Rex through the fence with his teeth oozing with spit. "Hey" Mark yelled, "Come on in!" I ran inside and sat on a brown leather chair. "Here's his dog food, he said handing me a big blue bag. "He needs to be fed twice a day and you can let him out three times every day." "Anything else?" I asked. "Nope, just don't take him off his chain." Mark ran out the door, and drove off with his parents. I walked home and thought "this won't be so bad after all."

The next morning my mom drove me to Mark's house on her way to the grocery store. I got out of the car and ran inside the house. I picked up his food bowl and went to the back door. I opened it just a crack and peeked outside and there was Rex laying on the grass looking like he was going to cry. I walked over to him and put the food bowl on the ground. I unhooked the chain and…it was the worst mistake of my life. Rex darted toward me and ripped my pants, again! I was furious, but so was he. I ran to the fence and started to climb it. Jumped over it and my shoe fell off. I watched as he ripped the laces to shreds.

I ran home screaming like a girl. I bought Rex a shock collar and I am never going to feed him again. So now Mark asks Jimmy, a strong kid to feed him. I'll stick with my bunnies even though I love dogs. That day was truly the worst time I helped someone.

3

The Bus Incident

Have you ever helped somebody that almost cost you your entire life! I have. In fact, it taught me an important lesson. Never fight the school bully when he's annialating the school nerd in the school bus. Because that lead to everyone including the bus driver to get really dang injured. So this is how the nightmare began. It was seven thirty am., and of course I was sleeping in my bedroom when all of a sudden ding, ding, ding! I quickly got up while screaming like a girl! I looked at my calendar and saw to it that it was Monday. Then furios sounds punched my door. Then someone said, hey loser, get your clothes on, the bus is outside. I immediately knew the voice was my no good can't get a job except torment me for eternety big brother. So I put on my clothes and walked toward the bus not knowing the danger that was awaiting me. When I got in the bus, I sat on the nearest bench. Since my house was so far away from my school, it usually took 35 minutes to get there. And that was enough time for people like Sam Jones. a.k.a. "The school Bully" to bully. And it couldn't have been a better day with Lonnie Tover, a.k.a. "The school Nerd" in the bus. When probably fifteen minutes passed, Sam walked toward Lonnie. When Lonnie looked up he was all of a sudden feriosly punched in the face! Everyone and I got up to see the comotion. Lonnie was on the floor bleeding and begging Sam to stop. But he would'nt he would keep hitting him like he was a punching bag. I was nervous. Not for me, but for Lonnie. He was getting beat up so brutally. So in my mind, I had two options. Eather save him and probably lose my face. Or watch. I was gonna pick option two, but I could'nt. I picked option one. I ran to Sam and before he can catch an eye on me...boom!! I kicked him so hard that he flew in the air to a bench. Then the bus driver walked over to my position and said what happened. Nothing I said nervously hiding Lonnie behind my back. Okay he said as he got a candy from his pocket. Then my eyes opened big. I said, sir who's driving the bus. Why me. Oh oh he said nervously. Boom!!! The bus brutally crashed through a tree. I opened my eyes after I was knocked out. Ah man I said as everyone was moaning. How is everyone the bus driver said the next day. Good we lied. Well I garantee there will be no problems today. I got up and saw 3 cats and a dog heading our way! Oh no. Here we go again! I better get another cast for my other leg!

4

As I walked down the hallway, I saw two girls pushing. I thought one of the girls was going to be mean to the other girl.

When I sat down by my classroom I read for about 15 minutes. As the clock went tick-tock I read some more. When the bell rang I put my book up, and went into the classroom. I scampered to my desk a girl named Anna and Kerrie sat by me. Kerrie was there, but Anna wasn't there. I thought she was tardy. "Knock, knock." "Come in," said Mrs. Bell. Anna came in. She was red in the face. She sat down in her desk and did her work.

When it was lunchtime, Anna stole Kerrie's lunch money. So Kerrie had to have peanut butter and jelly sandwich. Kerrie couldn't eat the sandwich because she was allergic to peanut butter. When we went out to recess I asked Anna if she stole Kerrie's lunch money. She said "No" in a mean way. Before I could say anything else our lunch teacher Mrs. Web told us to line up. When we got back to the class we had to go to the library. Mrs. Bell told Kerrie and me to stay in the classroom because we had no books. I told Kerrie to look for her money. I helped her look in the desks, cabinets, and tubs. There was no money anywhere. When the class got back the bell rang, and we had to leave.

We got on the bus and went home. Anna, Kerrie, and I were the first stop. When we got off Anna said, "Never push me again," and she pushed Kerrie to the ground. She was blushing and crying. I helped her up. I noticed Anna's book bag was open so I pushed her. Quickly I took her book bag off and dumped everything out. Kerrie and I tore papers, crumbled her homework, and we went through her textbooks, and we couldn't find the money. We dumped everything out of her pencil box. We found the money, and we said, "Now you pick up the rest of your stuff, Anna." That was the greatest time helping someone.

I used to think people could handle things on their own. Now they can't always handle things by themselves.

5

The Melon Lolypop

Do you have a time when you helped someone? Well I do, and I just happened to save their life while doing it.

It all happened on one fine spring morning. The birds were singing and the sun was smiling down. Josie and I were having a blast on the trampoline. Woopie! Josie's brown pigtails were flying everywhere as she jumped higher and higher trying to touch the clear, blue sky while sucking on her melon flavered lolypop. I was about to comment on how her pink plaid skirt clashed with her yellow tank top when she did a front flip for me. That was when the happy day changed.

"Wow Josie, that was amasing," I said half twirling, half dancing across the trampoline. When she didn't respond I turned to take a look at her. Josie's face was purple and her brown eyes were bulging. The lolypop had disappered and her hands were clenched around her neck.

At first I thought she was kidding, but then I relised this was no joke. Josie was choking! Suddenly I had a flash back. I was little and watching Scooby Doo. Shaggy was choking till Fred came and pushed around his middle. Returning from my flash back I relised what I had to do. Bouncing to Josie I placed my hands around her waist and pushed. Finnally, after about 30 seconds a slimy green lolypop fell to the floor. After Josie got her breth back she hugged me to deth and promised to never, ever suck a lolypop again while jumping. I told her I was just glad she was alive.

You may help someone with homework or teach them to read, but I saved someones life on a trampoline.

6

BBEEEEPPP!! It was Saturday morning at exactly 7:14 a.m. I got up, went to the dining room, and a chocolicious smell came from the kitchen. I saw my mom and dad cooking breakfast. "Who wants chocolate chip pancakes? I want you and Talia to have a good breakfast – remember we're going to Travis Park Church to feed the homeless, said Mom in a exciting tone. "Aw, can't I just stay home and watch TV?" I replied. "No, you're going," exclaimed Dad.

Before I knew it, we were in our old Mercury mini-van on our way to downtown San Antonio. I was still half-asleep until I heard about 10 honks. When a car ran a red light, Dad slammed the brakes – it sounded like fingernails on a chalkboard: a bad, bad, bad sound.

When we entered the church, we saw our friends, the Moore family. They help feed the homeless too. They led us to the kitchen, where there were 9 or 10 other people. Talia, and Perry (the Moore's daughter) made the pancakes and I slapped on the fake buttery substance. Before we went to the serving room, we all washed our hands and exchanged a prayer.

As we walked slug-like into the room, I peered into the ajoining hall where the homeless people were. There were a lot. Curran, the Moore's son and I got into our positions as syrup-pourers and everybody else got in their places such as servers, or drink giver-outers.

The people started to "invade" the room where the food was. We were serving pancakes, a egg-cassrole, sausage and bacon. Some of the people were scary looking, some nice, and even some that looked like you and me that were just looking for a free meal. There was this one person that was in a wheel chair, and he was blind, so he had a dog with sunglasses on it was hilarious! When people came to get syrup, they were sometimes not understandable, so I poured either too much or too little.

My dad took me on a tour of the church at the end. I saw doctors, showers, and clothes that are all free, because they need them.

On the way home I asked my mom and dad, "Can we do this again? It makes me feel like I can really help people." Mom replied, "Of course."

Pancake Helper

"Time for Breakfast!" My mom yelled. My little brother, Braulio; My big sister, Araceli; and I, Betsy were all sitting quietly at the dinning room waiting for my dad, Martin, to get home from work and my Mom, Areelia, to make breakfast. "Betsy, come help me with the pancakes!" My mother comanded. I had never suspected that I was going to use the stove because I'm only 5¾ years old and I'm barley allowed to use it. "But Mother, I'm a bit to young to use the stove, don't you think?" I asked her. "But, Betsy, you are only going to help me by getting the batter ready." mother exclaimed. So I got the pancake mix, the milk, the eggs and mixed it all up with the whisk. Although the pancake mix stuck to the bowl and it was hard to get off. My mom told me to mix the batter for five more minutes. My brother was getting mad because he wanted his pancakes…..and my sister as well.

My mom turned on the stove while I was getting ready to stop mixing. "And presto!" I said joyfully. There was a beige, bubbly liquid after I was all done mixing. I asked my mother if that's how it was supposed to look and she said "Yes!"

I saw my mom as she poured the batter into the pan and started flipping and turning the pancakes until they were ready to eat. She put them all in a big, round plate beside her. Although a few got burnt and she noticed that they were pretty small too.

I thought that with the batter that was left I could make a big daddy pancake for my dad when he came back from work. My mom had to stand really close to me so that I would not get burnt. Like I said I'm only 5¾ so I have to stand on a stool to reach the stove. My big daddy pancake was HUGE. I would have never finish the pancake if it was for me!

Finally, my dad came home with a big appitite. We all sat down, prayed our blessings, and started eating our yummy pancakes.

Even though we made a mess I was surprised that my first time using the stove I didn't get burnt. Plus, I had loads of fun and I learned that making pancakes costs a lot of TLC (Tender love, and care.) Now you know that this is one of the funnest times I've helped someone and now I'm mom's little helper.

8

"I'm board," moand Kate. "Me too," said Neal. "Me three," whined Erik. "Hey," I exclaimed. "Why don't we go outside!" "That's a great idea," said Erik as he scurried to his room to put his shoes on. Then from outside we all heared a loud "Meeoow." We rushed outside and found Lucy, our cat, with a bird in her mouth warning Lila, our other cat, to stay away from her catch. "Daddy, come quickly!" yelled Kate. "Lucy caught a babby bird!" He ran outside and started to make Lucy drop the bird. She eventually dropped it and ran off. "I think it's dead," whisperd Neal. We went inside with the bird to see if it still lived. I was so sad for the bird, I ran to my room and started crying.

--"Peeep!" I heared and ran down the hall to the living room. Everybody was laughing. The young bird had survived. "Maybe he's hungry," Kate told us. So, we got some cat food and water, mixed it together so it was nice and mushy and fed it to the young bird. "Can we name him!?" I exclaimed. "I guess so, Emma," mumbled my dad. "Yeah!" we all yelled. "But, we'll have to let him go sooner or later." "Aww," we whined.

That afternoon, I helped my dad make a temporary home for the little guy. We got a big bucket and filled it with grass, twigs, and some leaves so he would be comfortable. Then we placed the young bird in his home and then put the bucket in the garage so the cats wouldn't get him again. I then went inside to think of a name for him. "What are ya doin'?" asked Neal. "Trying to think of a name for that bird," I answered. "How about Bob," Neal exclaimed. "Naaw, I don't think he'll like it," I exclaimed. "Since when do birds care about their names?," Neal asked. "I du know," I mumbled. "I know," I yelled. "Micky!" "Great," exclaimed Neal. "Let's go tell the others."

The next morning, we went to go check on Micky and to feed him. He seemed to be alright so my dad said, "Today we should let Micky go." None of us wanted to but we knew it was the right thing. So, my dad went to the garage to get him. He came out and gave him to me. "Here," he said. "You do it." I helled him up high and waited. Soon I felt him stand up and in the blink of an eye, he flew off. I felt good but at the same time, sad. "I"ll never forget Micky," said Kate. "Neither will I," I whisperd.

Sweet Sugar

Have you ever wondered what an ant would say if it could talk to you? I did, untill last Saturday. I not only talked to an ant, but I became an ant, and helped some of them gain the magical sugar they needed to survive and it's all because of a toy I made..

It all started upstairs in my room. I was making my invention called the shrink-o-ray. I was just putting the final touch on it when it occurred to me that I needed to test it before I went off and vapored about it. I decided to test out on my mirrer, because that was the one thing in my room I didn't need. I stood in front of my mirror and shot, but as soon as it hit the mirror it bounced of the mirror and headed strait toward me! "Oh No," I thought. "This can't be good." I tried to side step, but I was to late. It hit me square in the chest, and before I knew it my room had grown the size of a skyscraper. "At least it worked," I thought to myself as I slid down the rainpipe and down into the lawn.

I thought I would land nicely on a blade of grass, but instead I landed face first in a pile of dirt. ("Owww!") I think my fall must have had a ripple efect because, suddenly, all of the pile fell down onto me. I felt like one million cars were squishing down on me. After some struggling, I was able to move again. Finding the outside of the dirt was like finding an elephant in a haystack, easy, so it didn't take very long. Once I was out I decided to walk around. I slid down a grass blade from the top of the pile. "Now, this is a new milieu," I thought, for I had never seen the lawn from this point of veiw. I looked around at the blades that probably were as tall to me as the beanstalk was to Jack. Suddenly, these red things came up to me. I started to feel warmer. "Fire ants!" I screamed. I ran past them at the speed of a race car. After a few minutes, I turned around to see if they were chasing me, and suddenly fell into a big hole. I looked around and saw that I had fallen into an ant mound. I dicided to look around but just as I was rounding a corner two fire ants grabbed me from behind and tied me up! They took me, all tied up, blindfolded, and gagged to their queen. They took my blindfold off so that I could see her. She looked just like all the rest, except that she had a golden crown on her head. As soon as she saw me she gasped. "Are you the one with the shirnk-o-ray?" she asked. I nodded my head, and the two ants behind me gasped. "Leya!" she called. A girl that looked exactly like her came into the room. Then, the queen rolled out this story about magical sugar that the ants needed to survive. "OK," I said. "I'll find the sugar."

The next day, Leya (the princess) and I set out on our journy. The first few hours were smooth but the tenth one we ran into giant cockroaches. The princess told me to make a parachute out of grass, and we got past them. A few minutes later we had found the sugar. I took a bite, and it tasted like apple crisp. I was suddenly big again, so I carried the whole bowl back. I dumped it into the mound. I was glad I had helped someone.

I have one more thing to tell you. Last Saturday, I won the annual best lie and fib story too!

Baby-sitting Jake

It starts out Thursday Feb. 9 when my mama and I were eating pizza and watching Back to the Future II, when the phone rang. "Ring." My mom picked it up first. "Hello" she said. And after 30 min. my mom said "Ok. I'll ask him." And hung up the phone. "Ok, if this is the least of how much girls talk on the phone, god only knows how much girls talk the most," I thought not speaking it. "Who was that?" I asked curiously. "Libby Bently," my mom answered. "Why did she call," I asked. "Well she, Rob, your father and I are going to the theatre tomorrow. And Carlile and Jake are going to spend the night here. And that's not all, you can take care of Jake and keep him out of the girls hair for ten dollars. So what do you say?" said my mom. "Ok," I grumbled. And I called Libby to tell her my decision.

After the long day at school when I got home I started thinking about what to do with Jake. But when dad came home I asked him, "Can we go to Hollywood video to get movies for Jake and I?" He said "Yes" but when we got there I didn't know what to get because Jake is five and he can't watch what I watch like Stephen King's movies. So I got something that I would never of thought to watch Ice Age 2.

So when Jake and Carlile's mom and dad came I told them what I was going and they agreed. When dinner was finished we waited for the girls babysitter to keep them out of our hair. When she came Jake and I started watching our movie. When it was finished I turned to regular TV. I started watching Disney channel because Jake couldn't watch cartoon network and then I asked Jake "What do you want to watch?" He didn't reply. I asked him again. Still no reply. Then I crouched over to see what he was doing and he was…sleeping. "I had watched 3 hours of stuff I didn't want to watch for him and he was sleeping," I thought to myself. But then I got to watch and do what I wanted. This is the easiest ten dollars I ever made. I'm having fun and making money. What could be better," I thought. But after a while we had to go to bed.

In the morning we all got up and started watching TV. Then Libby came to pick up Carlile and Jake and to pay me. After they left, I thought "That was easy and fun and I got payed. I should help people like this more often.

11

Many people would have wrote about helping a old lady or helping your mom out, but as I sit on the back porch I'll tell a time when I helped a dog and in return that dog helped me.

I was probably 6 or 7 years old and we had a poodle named Sophie. She was very old but still as frisky as a baby poodle. We were playing in the back yard doing fetch and playing with my sister Avery. But then we had to leave for school. Avery put Sophie up as I ran and got my backpack. then when I got home my mom looked really sad. I asked,"what was the matter?! She replied, "Sophie is very old Ellery. She cannot see well or hear well. She is very very old and we may have to help her." I asked "What in the world do you mean?! She answered very soloemnly, "Ellery dear we…have to put Sophie to a very long rest. I gasped in horror, shock, and sadness. You do not mean put her to sleep.

I was very calm but then a bubble of outrage started to emerge! I screamed and yelled we can't no way no no no why we can't Meanie! I screamed and ran to my room, slammed the door and threw myself on my bed and started balling.

Then I started to think. I thought maybe it's best for her. But no matter what I thougt it didn't seem fair, it just didn't seem right.

The next day there was nothing I could do to stop it…they put her to sleep. And as I remember that day just as it was yesterday I remember the smell of wet fur she had the curly yet soft texture of fur and most of all her little yappy bark. I watch the sunset and clutch my other dog Felici and say aloud, "We helped her and in return she helped me to grow up and face the truth but yet I still don't want it to happen again…to you."

Dear Steven,

Remember when I was about 5 years old and you taught me everything there was to know about baseball? If you don't that's okay because it'll be with me forever.

It was a hot Saturday afternoon and your team was scheduled to practice. I thought I'd tag along just for the fun of it. I sat on the bench as you went off the field and started getting loose. I just sat around looking at everything around me. This was my first time being at an actual field and I was amazed. The freshly cut grass, the white bases and the soft, red dirt. It was everything you said it would be. As I was watching you dad came over and said "I knew you'd like it, how would you like to touch the field?" He picked me up and set me down on the soft grass and I ran around the bases. When I got to home I looked at dad and a small tear ran down his eye as he said "Steven did the exact same thing when I took him out here for the first time."

Dad grabbed me and took me off the field and said "We've got to practice so sit and enjoy." I watched you snag ground balls and thought "That's my big brother, the best player alive." I got up and did everything you did. You looked at me and gave me a grin and tipped your hat. I had a smile that reached ear to ear. I left the bench for a little while and went exploring. I went onto another field and pretended to be in the pros. I ran around all of the bases and acted if I had just hit a homerun and my teammates were waiting for me at home plate. I layed on the bench and started dozing off.

Dad came over, shook me and said "Your brother has a surprise for you on the field." I ran as fast as I could over to you but nothing was with you. I look all over until finally dad said "It's behind him." I went behind you and that's when I saw it…my very own glove. I stood there in shock and disbelief. You looked at me and said "It was mine when I was little."

We played baseball for a little while and you taught me the basics. Ever since then you practiced with me everyday until I got better and better. Now my whole life is revolved around baseball. I've won two city-wide championships, MVP of an all star team, and I owe it all to you. Steven if you wouldn't have helped me from when I was 5 to today I don't know where I would've ended up. I just wanted to tell you thanks and there's nothing in the whole world that I could repay you with.

13

Music, I guess it's just in my blood. I have a passion for it like no other. Starting out was a piece of cake, but I had to face many obstacles to get to where I'm at today. Sitting at the piano for the first time, feeling nervous about learning how to play I remember thinking, "Can I do this?"

A feeling of apprehension rushed through my body. This was going to be my first music lesson. My mom and I soon arrived at the music teacher's home. "Hi, I'm Mrs. Richling," the woman said. "I'm Maria," I responded with a big grin on my face. The thirty minutes I was there seemed to go by quick. I learned all the basic material for a beginner. Once every week I would go back and have a thirty minute lesson with her. As the school year began I started going to Mrs. Schlaudt, my music theory teacher's home. There I was with about six other kids my age, with whom I learned music theory with throughout the year.

Before I knew it a year had passed and I had two years of piano experience. That whole year went the same, except that I had to have a certain number of pieces memorized. In the end I would eventually play them in front of a judge that would critique me. During that same year I entered the Reflections program where I wrote a piece, that won honorable Mention at District and State levels. My third year went quickly before my eyes I continued working hard and memorized six pieces by the end of the year. Last year was my fourth year playing I once again did my best and won Honorable Mention at District and State levels. I am currently working on my fifth year and trying to accomplish great rewards by doing something I love and do well at.

Playing the piano is very important to me. Music is something I take very seriously. After all the hard work, effort, and time I've put into it I won't be quitting anytime soon. But it all works out in the end when you're rewarded for something you do best at.

14

Have you ever wanted to hit someone so hard that it knocked them out? I don't know about you, but I have! This is the reason that my mom joined me into volleyball. No matter how much she doubts it, I know it's true. When I started out playing volleyball, I wasn't exactly the best volleyball player on the team. Actually, I was more like the worst volleyball player in the history of sports! I couldn't bump, set, serve, or spike the dang ball. Being this horrible made me determined to play…and I mean really play! So hard that I would be sweaty and stinky and my hair would be all messed up and everything when I walked out of that gym at the end of practice time. One day, I don't know what came over me, I just began to workout like crazy. Believe me, working out those arm and back muscles made me the strongest hitter and overhand server on my team. I felt like I was on top of the world, nobody could get in my way! Then it hit me, it takes more than just spiking and overhand serving to be a great volleyball player. Duh! My mother was one of the greatest volleyball players of her time, therefore I asked her if she could help me…and do you know what she said, "I think you can do this on your own." Of course, I begged her until she gave up and said yes. Hey, what are daughters for anyways, if not to bug you to death? We jogged all the way from our house to the courts. That day my mom taught me a lot about how to play volleyball the right way. I learned how to bump, set, and underhand serve! I was finally becomming an alright volleyball player. Finally, a huge tournament came up on my calendar. When the team arrived at the college where we would be playing, we stretched and started warming up. I heard a voice blasting out from the intercom, "Let the games begin!" All of a sudden, my stomach went into knots, I was serving first! The team spreaded out on the court and I walked over to the serving position. The whistle blew and I threw the ball up into the air…we scored! Butterflies filled my stomach and all of a sudden I felt numb all over my sweaty, little body. I served one point after another, but no one could seem to return my speedy serves. I could feel the air around me move when I tossed up the ball and then hit it with all the power I had in my body. Point after point we kept scoring! I bet the other girls on my team were becomming bored after a while. Before I knew it the game was over and all because of my serves, we won! Don't you just love taking all your anger out on that day.

"Dear Matt, so I'm really glad we go out I mean I ♥ it when we're together. You're soo fun to be around, and cute, too. Ooh a double threat lol." Well yah, I don't think I'll be sayin that anymore cause we're…well…let's put it this way we're not as close as we used to be. Do you remember how, where, when, and why it happened? I think you do. But let me tell you the story from my point of view. Okay so I had just come over and we were "watching a movie" lol. But, my mom said I had to come home. Right as you were about to walk me home Ben called remember? He said he was almost there so you couldn't walk me home right then. I got a little upset but it didn't bother me much. So I waited until Ben got there. While you and him were talking in the living room, I got your phone and looked at your messages and one said "Hey …I didn't want it to be weird but I've had a crush on you since the beginning of the year." OMG! Wait. What?! No it can't be. But I had evidence in front of my very eyes and I knew they weren't deceiving me. I didn't know what to do. I was scared. Tears started running down my face. Oh no!! I put your phone down and fell on your bed. You walked in and said, "What's wrong?" but I didn't say anything. I just stared at you with tears pouring down my face. You pulled me 2 you and just held me in your arms. I guess you didn't know what to say, cause it got really quiet. You asked me what's wrong again but I didn't answer. I just said I have to go home. Of course your mom made you walk me home. On the way it was very quiet I couldn't hear anything except the sniffling of my nose because I was crying, and the sound of our shoes walking on the pavement. Once again you asked me what was wrong and I said "I don't like how you lie." What!" you said and I stopped talking. When we came on my street I said, "I got it now, you don't have to walk any further." So you turned around and I kept on walking. I came up to my house and my whole family was doing something different outside. I had tears in my eyes so they asked me what was wrong and I told them I ran and twisted my ankle. They believed me so I just walked to my room. You IM-ed txting me What's wrong? And I finally said it's about the txt mssges. And you said "No I said HAD a crush" but I didn't have one (and now I realize how stupid I was for not believing you). I stopped txting and went to sleep. The next day at school I didn't say a word to you at all. I didn't even stand by you. And that's when the badness started and I mean for real. I felt really bad so when I got home I asked you if you wanted to go to the school basketball game with me so we could talk but you said b-ball isn't your thing. I started to think it was just an excuse but I went anyways to see my friends. I was txting you on the way there and when I was there all hell broke loose somehow we got onto a subject that I didn't want to deal with . "Are you saying you don't want to be with me anymore?" and you said "it might be better off that way cause I mean you're shy I'm outgoing and we do need to get to know each other better." Hold on!! Rewind. What did he just say? Nah. No way. Whatever! I kept trying to deny the fact that you were about to break-up. The next thing I know I got a txt that said "so I guess we're not BF and GF anymore." I could feel the hotness in my eyes as the tears started to flow. Everybody around me knew what was happening so when they saw me cry they held me so tight. I ran to the bathroom. All the lights were off. I tried to look at myself in the mirror but it was too dark. So I just stood there and cried. Bai ran in, grabbed me so tight. She just kept talking and telling me it would be alright. But I did not believe that! Why?! I kept asking myself, why? If only I would've done this and not have said that maybe we would still be 2gether. I kept making regrets that before that moment I would've never regretted. In my mind right then I was the stupidest person alive. OMG! I swear I was hyperventilated of something cause I couldn't breathe. I didn't know what to do. Well the game ended and my mom picked me up. I got home, ran to my room and started writing, about everything. I finally stopped writing and fell asleep listening to our song. The next morning getting ready for school I made sure that I got your CD that you let me borrow. I finished getting ready and my mom drove me to school. When we were almost there she asked me how we were doing and I just shook my head no and the tears started pouring again. She said, "I'm sorry, sweetie, but I still ♥ you." I got out of the car and walked up to everybody. They started asking me if I was OK and I was like yah. I came up to you and handed you your CD, then walked away. NOTHING ELSE IS that clear except I spent the next 3-4 weeks crying every night. It's been 3 ½ months and I'm learning to forget about it, cause it doesn't help if you stress over something like that. Now like I said I am starting to forget but every time I think you're gone you come back again. I don't know if it'll ever happen again so in the meantime I'll be learning how to forget about you and I.

16

Have you ever had something outrageous happen to you? Well, I have. I have lived in an orphanage since I was six weeks old. My mom dropped me off the porch because she didn't want me. Just thinking about how she didn't want me makes me feel like there was an emptiness in my stomach. As much as I try to forgive her for doing that, I can't.

Today was the day in the orphanage where a whole bunch of families come and pick a child to take home and keep for a couple of weeks to see if they like them. I hate it with all my heart. In my opinion the families think of it as buying a pair of shoes; you have to try them on to see if you are going to buy them. That is not what it is like at all; you're actually dealing with a real person with real feelings. I have only been taken home once because I'm not that pretty. I'm plain faced, tall and skinny, my face is freckled, and my hair looks like a rats nest. My only redeeming quality is my big brown eyes. That was the worst feeling I had ever had when those people took me back because they said I wasn't pretty enough.

Now that I am twelve years old my job is to look after the little ones. Seeing them go day by day hurts me inside because I've been here for twelve years, and they have only been here for a few years and they already get to leave this prison. On holidays, it is hard for me seeing everybody getting presents from relatives. Then me receiving nothing.

Another year has passed and it is still the "same old same old." Except for the fact that I am thirteen now, and I have outgrown all of my clothes. My pants are two inches too short and my shirts are so short they show my stomach. When we go out in public people stare at me like I am a three headed monster. It's very embarrassing to work around looking like you are wearing your eight year old sister's clothes, but it's not my fault I can't afford to buy new ones.

It had been two weeks since the last family adopted somebody. The headmaster said that today another family was coming and to get our best clothes on. Well I didn't have any that were too swift; but I managed. When they came we all went out into the hall. To my surprise they picked me. I was too happy for words. Their names were Tom and Jill. They were so nice and they liked me and told me I was pretty and that they loved me. That was the most outrageous thing I have ever experienced, and I loved them back so they decided to keep me. I think now that I have Tom and Jill, I can forgive my mom.

17

The one thing I've learned to do well is cope with loss, stress, and deprivement of my little brother and grandmother. They were in the World Trade Center the day it was bombed. The pain of not finding their bodies is even worse. My fifty three year old grandmother and eight year brother were innocent victims of terror. Which leaves me wondering W-H-Y!

They had won a trip to Manhattan, New York off the radio. The first day they arrived, my brother suggested that we go site seeing, my grandmother fully agreed. They called us every waking moment. This day was September 11, 2001. On that day I knew in my three year old little heart that they would return just as they had left, but was I wrong.

On September 10, 2001, they set out to have a day on the town. "That was the best day ever both of them had remarked on the phone. Then Nanny said, "Since it's Cooper's birthday tomorrow, I've planned a floor-to-floor tour of the Twin Towers as a present." A day and tour that my family and will soon never forget.

September 11, 2001, my brother is turning nine. A day that is always filled with happiness, excitement, and joy and it would turn out to be a dreadful, horrifying day of pain and misery. My brother was so excited about today that it seemed like he had won a million dollars for his good looks.

They were going up to the 88th floor when all of a sudden everything stops! The elevator, the people, everything…STOPS! Then B-O-O-M!! All you hear are screaming, terrified people all around you. Then the guy they met coming in the elevator phone rings. The caller on the other says, "A plane has just crashed through the side of the North wall!" They were all bewildered!

We were all enjoying some television when the phone rang with the devastating news. My mother answers the phone and says, "Hello." At that same moment it seemed mother's whole world came tumbling down with just a couple words from a stranger. Only one person survived in the elevator full of 30 people. His name was Earl, he could only identify three people, my brother and grandmother and a co-worker.

I believe that both my grandmother and brother are watching after me in the heavens above.

This event was a tragic one for history, but a life changing one for my family and I. We had one of the most challenging moments in our lives on September 11, 2001. A very memory is all we have of Cooper Casaubon and Cindy Brooks, my loving brother, and my grandmother.

Emily Champagne – Grade 7 – Glenn Middle School, San Angelo ISD

I was sitting next to my third grade teacher's giant bookcase on a bean bag, reading an "I Spy" magazine, when a book high upon a shelf caught my eye. It had the most beautiful cover with a picture of a girl and a half goat, half man holding an umbrella. A great shining lamppost illuminated their faces and the snowflakes falling all around. I said to myself, "I have to read this book," and from that day on I was hooked!

Yes, in third grade I was an avid reader, maybe only of skinny, thirty page beginner chapter books, but I still read! My mother encouraged me to read past a second grade level, but I refused. That was, until I discovered the "magical bookcase".

The bookcase was all the way up to the ceiling in Mrs. Baker's classroom and it was about six feet long. One day, while reading an "I Spy" magazine I noticed a book with a beautiful cover, it was "The Lion, the Witch, and the Wardrobe", by C.S. Lewis, who was soon to become one of my most favorite authors. I borrowed the book and came back the next day, eager for more.

I started to read the next book out loud to my little sister, but I stumbled along the words and got so frustrated that I made myself cry. The thing is, I didn't give up, and I tried everyday until I taught myself to read well out loud. A few good books read aloud made me want to read more and more! I thought of it as if my brain was like a sponge, always wanting to soak up more and more information. In sixth grade I took a reading level test to see exactly how much information I had soaked up, and I'm proud to say that I read on a grade twelve reading level, all thanks to me learning how to read aloud!

My sixth-grade reading teacher read my class the kid version of "Hamlet". I enjoyed it so much that I checked out the original version at the library and came back the next day with thoughts of the irony in the book swirling around in my head. I then started reading Edgar Allen Poe's stories, starting with "The Black Cat", and on to "The Telltale Heart". I was amazed by the way Poe had spun the tales of lies and horror. By the end of his stories I was guaranteed to be on the edge of my seat. Some stories were quite confusing, others I had figured out from the beginning. Poe's stories taught me how to create a twisted plot and a story that others would like to read. Because of Poe, I'm an author!

Thanks to all the books I've read, and those who taught me to read aloud, I have the good skills that have helped me to write great stories, and it all started with a book about a brave lion, an incredibly awful witch, and a simple, yet very important wardrobe!

19

Dear Reader,

If I have learned how to do anything well, it's cope with life. I've had a couple of curve balls thrown at me that I thought I could never dodge. Everyone knows, "life is hard," but sometimes it gets a little too hard!!

I remember days I wouldn't do anything but lie between my covers and bawl the whole day, because my parents were into it or daddy "went out for some fresh air." I couldn't stand to see my parents arguing. One day, the arguing got so bad that my father moved out for about a week. I know that's nothing compared to some people whose parent(s) moves out or leaves for years at a time, but that's what it felt like….years.

Times really got hard when our money was low and we didn't have enough to pay the month's rent. Our landlord let us slide a couple of times until she couldn't anymore…we got an eviction notice.

When we had to move, we were stuck because we didn't have anywhere to go. Luckily, my grandmother's arms were wide open to us. As soon as my parents got back on their feet, we got ourselves a house built. We had a big house with 3 bedrooms and 2 baths. A few years after moving, God gave us a little blessing, and his name is Gaylen Jr. He had the cutest little smile and eyes that could melt the sun. Life was great…UNTIL…another curve ball was thrown, and my father started to drink. He would stay out to different hours of the night every day of the week. We barely talked any more, I felt a separation between the two of us.

Sometimes I would go over to my grandma's house just to get away, but sometimes that wasn't the perfect place to be because my pa-pa would always be in a bad mood. I gave up, I rarely had anyone to talk to, I felt alone. Struggles brought me down, but I didn't let that keep my head hanging low, I found joy in reading…UNTIL…One day when my parents had a garage sale they sold all of my books. When my mom told me I was very upset. Even though she gave me the money they made from my books, I didn't have anything to keep my mind occupied.

This just goes to show learning to deal with people and life is darn hard, but always expect something to go wrong. I'm not saying you should be pessimistic towards life, just don't get your hopes up too much.

Love, Qua'Shayla Cobb

I was sitting on my bed, staring at my trophies when I thought to myself, "I want another trophy so bad, but I'm exhausted!" I was about two minutes into a deep sleep, when suddenly my bedroom door flew open. A strange figure walked in, said something, then turned around and left in a hurry. "Could I be dreaming," I thought, "or could this actually be happening?"

It was spring break and I was living the life. Got up whenever, and stayed home all day. It just didn't get any better than that. That was day two out of my seven day break, or should I say nightmare. Day three was worse! The next morning I woke up and ate. Then I casually walked up to my dad and asked, "Dad, can you teach me how to play volleyball as good as you?" "I can certainly try," he replied! He went with me to the gym and we started playing. At first I was terrible, but then after a couple of hours I was starting to get the hang of it. After our four hour practice, I was worn out. Then my dad said to me, "OK dear, we'll practice again tomorrow for another four hours." I was so tired that didn't want to practice for a very long time. "OK dad."

The next day, I was so sore that I could barely move, but I still got up and went to practice. This exact schedule went on until day five. On day five, I was so sore that I played sick so I wouldn't have to go. My dad actually believed me, so he went to work while I was "sick." After he left I was back to normal. I was on the phone with my friend Kassidy when he walked into my room. "I'll have to call you back," I said to Kassidy. "Feeling better?", my dad asked me in a mean tone. I shook my head as I was feeling guilty. "I gave up my time to help you because you asked me to. Practice makes perfect. If you don't practice, you won't get any better. Oh yeah, by the way, we were supposed to play a volleyball game tomorrow against other people, but I guess you don't want to. Think about it", he said. As he walked out the door I could see a tear rolling down his face. I knew he was disappointed in me. "What have I done?", I asked myself. My dad had left and wouldn't be back for a while. Then I realized that it was my dad I saw entering and leaving my room in my dream.

Suddenly I had a brilliant idea. I made a few phone calls and everything was set. I would play tomorrow with my dad, and my friends were coming over to practice with me. The next day my dad and I went to the game. Before we played I apologized for lying to him, and he forgave me. Then he said, "Let's kick some butt." At about 11:00 a.m. we had won in our division and in our group. We each left the game with trophies. When I got home I put my trophy on my shelf and said, "I'm glad I kept going!"

"Practice makes perfect", is a good saying but, "Never give up", to me, is an even better saying!

21

Have your parents ever given you any great advice? Well, mine have! When I was about five or six my mom told me to always chase my dreams, if it was something that I really wanted. She was inspiration, and I knew that I would always follow her advice. When I got older, my mom became very ill. I didn't understand and what was going on. I mean she was my mom! I didn't think that the world would ever take her away from me! But, I was wrong. On the day of January 21, 1998, my mom passed away. It was one of the saddest days of my entire life.

I grew up some and finished school, I was given a scholarship and was accepted into Harvard Law School when I was twenty-one. My mom always told me to chase my dreams! I became one of the best lawyers that you could find around this place. However, I still had more dreams that needed chasing.

I wanted a family. I mean who doesn't love kids? One day at the supermarket, I met the love of my life. He was a dentist who had never been married before. We fell deeply in love and we thought we had it all.

Three years later we are still happily married with two amazing kids. My mom always told me to chase my dreams! I had all that I had ever wanted and owed it all to my mom. She was and still is the greatest person. She has a heart of gold and is the most selfless person that you will ever meet. I owe my entire life to her and would give it all up in a second for her. I that I have made her proud, because she always told me chase my dreams!

Sky Davis– Grade 7 -- Herman Furlough Middle School, Terrell ISD

Dear Dad,

Over the years you were never there for me. But one day when I least expected it something magical happened. You discovered the right path and wanted to be a better father. In the worst of times you dropped in and helped us. I was excited because you might have wanted to spend some time with your child. But even though I was happy to see you I was also scared because I had the feeling you were going to walk out on us again. These are the words I'm trying to say. I love you and I'm glad you have saved yourself to be a better person.

I was at home sleeping in my bed when you just happened to wake me up in the middle of a dream. You told me to get dressed and be ready in ten minutes. I didn't know what was happening but I obeyed your orders. I slipped in some jeans, put on a shirt, and tiptoed down the stairs to talk to you. Everything was a riddle and I couldn't fit the pieces together. I sighted you in the kitchen gulping down a glass of milk when you told me to get in the truck. The next thing that happened was shocking, but in a good way. I had walked outside and found fishing poles, but after that I was thinking, "I don't know how to fish."

Thirty minutes later after the drive we arrived at the lake. It expanded over one mile and as the sun rose the water glistened and created an image so beautiful that it felt like my sister was alive. After that feeling it was hard to get over but I managed. You parked the truck and we walked up to the dock dragging along the boat. "Let's get this thing in the water," you exclaimed. All of our gear was at one side and only room for two was left. Both of us gave a hard push and hopped in before it drifted away. It was time to catch some fish, but I didn't know how.

You handed me a pole with a worm on it, so I took a shot at a cast. Bam! The string flew 2 feet and slammed into the water. You laughed and said, "Let me show you." Your warm hands grabbed mine and showed me step by step. For the first time we were doing something together and I didn't want anything to ruin it. I threw my bait out in the water and waited. I felt a tug on the pole and yanked. The fish took off with the line and swam farther out. You grabbed on and we pulled him together. As soon as we got him in the boat he was a lot heavier. I pulled out the camera and took a picture.

After the fishing trip we got back home and I wanted to tell you something but I didn't. I'm glad you taught me how to fish or I would have never learned and we would of not been able to enjoy that life experience. Though it has been a while I now have the chance to tell you that I love you for all of the things you have done. I hope that you can live up to your name and help your family. This trip has made me realize how great it is to do things with you. Thank you for showing me how great being a father will be.

Your son,
Sky D.

Lucero DelaCruz– Grade 7 -- Herman Furlough Middle School, Terrell ISD

Dear Maritza,

Do you remember the time when we were in mom's car and that terrible accident had to happen. Well you wouldn't believe how guilty I felt ever since that day.

Like always we had to argue about where we were supposed to sit. I wanted to sit on mom's side and so did you. So then we started yelling at each others face. Mom had to stop us from yelling at each other. She also made me let you sit wherever you wanted to. After I traded you seats, I asked mom why did it always have to be whatever you say. She responded by saying that you were little and that you needed more attention. Her response made me so mad.

A few minutes later I looked at you and saw you looking out the window. I planned to grab you and move you to where I was sitting, so then I could sit where I wanted to. Suddenly, I grabbed you by your waist, and moved you over to the other side. While moving you to the other side, I heard something hit the other side door. I rapidly let go of you. Then you turned and looked at me. Your face was red and tears were rolling down your cheeks, but the thing that freaked me out the most was the blood dripping down your mouth.

Mom came inside the car rapidly when she heard your loud cry. She then asked me what had happened. After I was done telling her what had happened, she got mad and told me that I should be more careful with you, because you can get hurt easily. She still hadn't seen the blood you had in your mouth, and I was really scared to tell her.

While Mom was driving us back home, I asked you to open your mouth, so I could see what had happened. When you opened your mouth I saw that your front teeth were dislocated. That was the reason why you were bleeding so bad. I felt terrible down inside, because I knew it had been my fault. I then grabbed you in my arms and started crying, and telling you that I was really sorry, and that I loved you.

I decided it would be better if I told Mom. After I told Mom about your teeth, she stopped the car so she could take a look at it. When she saw you she also started crying. Then she started to panic, and couldn't find what to do. Then she decided to take you to the hospital. When we got to the hospital the doctor got a look at you, he said you were going to be okay in a couple of weeks, and that your teeth weren't going to fall out. I could see you were still in pain, and couldn't help feeling guilty and bad.

After that day I finally realized that you did need more attention and that I needed to be more careful with you because you are smaller and you can get hurt more easily. So this accident taught me a big lesson, and also taught me how to take good care of you. I also hope you don't have no hurt feelings against me, and that you understand that it was an accident, and that I didn't mean to hurt you in any kind of way.

24

Over the years, the word learning has had a huge effect on my sports career. All of my coaches have made me learn the ropes of the game, so I would be prepared. But, as a first time basketball player I had not learned how to do one important thing that all basketball players needed, and that is a good free throw.

On the night before the first game, I was very nervous, because I still had not figured out how to shoot a free throw. I had practiced numerous ways, but the ball was just not going in the hoop. As I layed in my bed, frustrated at the fact I couldn't shoot free throws, I thought, "I know the perfect person who could help me with this problem," I said, "Zach Lara!"

The next day my attitude had changed significantly because I knew Zach, who was the best shooter on the team, could help me. As my dad drove me up to the side of the gym, I saw all the basketball guys waiting for the door to open. I told my dad thanks and approached the guys. I saw Zach's tanned face through all the crowd. I knew telling him I couldn't shoot free throws would be embarrassing, but I knew it would be better than the torment I would get if I missed my free throws. I asked him if he would help me and he gladly accepted.

Coach Chavez opened the door and the team got ready. Me and Zach were the first ones on the court for "shoot around," so he could start teaching me. The lesson started out with me showing Zach how I shot. Right as I was about to shoot, he told me to freeze so I could correct my poor form. When Zach was done adjusting my form he told me to shoot. I was nervous but I bent my legs and shot. Sure enough, Zach was right. I did what he told me to and made my free throw. I thanked Zach and then told myself, "I did it, I learned how to shoot free throws!"

Learning to shoot these free throws was stressful but all worthwhile in the end. I strongly believe without Zach's help I would still be missing these shots. Learning is probably the best part of life.

My mom is short with short, wavy, brown hair. Her eyes are supposed to be green, but they always change colors according to her mood. She has always been there for me and always will be there for me. She has taught me many things I will always remember but one thing I truly treasure in my heart. How to read.

Sitting at our round table with a small pile of books for preschoolers, I thought, "I am going to read those."

"Now let's get started with words," said my mom, eager to teach me to read. "What is this word?" She pointed to a word in one of the sentences, in one of the books.

"That looks like, um, th-th-the, that's right, the," I said with confidence.

"Fabulous, let's do another," she cheered me on and pointed to another word in the same sentence.

"That one is, um, c-c-ca-car."

"Yes, correct," she told me with pride in her eyes. "Let's try the whole sentence now."

"The car d-d-drove d-dow-down the st-str-stree-street," I mumbled slowly, unsure if that was right.

"Wow, that was great for your first time ever reading a sentence." Her eyes were blue-green which meant she was happy.

I practiced about three sentences a day until one day my mom said, "I think, by the way you're reading, you will read great when you grow up. Now, I think you're ready to read a whole book, not just sentences."

I beamed with pride as she chose a book and sat down with me to read it.

"The dog is going for a long walk," I read. I finished the book, with reassurance from my mom, in about an hour.

Now that I'm older I can read a whole chapter book in about two to seven days. My mom reminds me all the time of her prediction of me reading great when I grew up, and her eyes turn blue-green with pride and happiness. She taught me to read, and I am so grateful that she is always there for me when I need her.

It was a nice summer day, about 80°, and slightly windy. The birds were singing and the flowers were blooming. In a small backyard in the middle of town was a big oak tree that stood about 75 feet tall. Under it, a middle-aged man and a child were shooting BB guns.

I was in my backyard, sitting in a green lawn chair, watching my dad easily shoot brown shotgun shells off of an Avon box. He shot all 5 shells off and handed me the BB gun, while saying it was my turn. He said I was out of bullets, and I thought, "What, do you expect me to reload it?" As it turns out he did. He showed me how to open the chamber near the end of the barrel and pour the bullets in. I got 2 or 3 in there, but spilt the rest. I looked to my dad for help, but he just said, "Pick them up, we don't have all day." I thought, "What kind of father is he? I have just touched a gun for the first time and I'm doing most of the work." I then picked up the bullets and carefully formed a funnel with my hands to pour them in. After that was done, I asked if there was anything else for me to do. He just laughed and said, "You'll see." As I closed the chamber on the barrel, I noticed it said "Remington." Consequently, I asked him what it was. He told me that it is a gun company that we buy all of our guns from. I then told him that I was going to get a better kind. He replied by insulting my shooting skills. Finally, he said there was one more thing to do. I ran over to the Avon box and set the shells up. As I was running back, he shot the box, knocking all of the shells down. I stopped right there and yelled, "What do you think you're doing?" He just smiled and said, "Pick them up." Right then I decided that on the way back I would stand in his line of fire so he couldn't knock the shells down. I did just that.

After he said I could shoot the BB gun, I went crazy. I started jumping up and down and yelling, "Yay, it's finally my turn!" I jumped up on the chair and asked for the gun. He immediately told me to get down and to settle down. After I was off the chair, he handed me the gun. Right after I had the gun I pointed it at the target, ready to shoot. My dad said not to shoot, and that I had to aim. On my first shot, I hit the fence. On my second shot, I hit the tree. On my third shot, I hit the box, but none of the shells fell down. My dad said to just keep trying. Finally, after about 30 shots, I hit the top of one shell. Then, before I could reload, he took the gun from me and shot the remaining 4 shells. I was amazed. My dad said, "Nothing is impossible, no matter how hard it may seem." At the time, I didn't know what that meant, but now I do. For the next year, I would go outside and shoot at the shells for several hours everyday. I got better week by week, and by the time I was 8, I shot very well. Patience is a virtue. If you want to do things with excellence, you must practice a lot. Also, responsibility is a huge part of life. If you act like I did with a weapon, you could hurt someone badly. Without patience, there is no excellence. Without excellence, life isn't worth living.

27

Dad, you are the most honorable person I know. You always knew what to do in a frantic situation, you always knew what to say to reason with someone, and you never show fear when the most fearful comes to you. You are the eye of the storm, and nothing can make you move, I thought until you left, then I realized who you really were.

When I was eight we moved into a bad neighborhood. Things weren't going well with Mom so you left. You left me there stranded on the island of becoming a man, all on my own with no tools to start the foundation, and no guild to show me the right way to do anything, so I had to do it myself. From that moment on, I was the one locking the doors at night, I was the last person awake making sure that all is well at night. I was the one holding Mom when she cried. I was the one pushing the car when it broke down, running errands, and calling the shots, defending the house from unwanted intruders, it was not you but me.

I learned to be patient, and strong. I learned to do the job well and to get the job done. I learned to pour my heart into things and give them all I've got. There was nothing too big for me to handle and nothing too small that could slide past my defenses. I was everything you weren't and a thousand times better that what you were. I am the man now. I am the one you'd go to if there was a problem, or a job needed to be done. I am sturdy and can only hold out through the strongest of storms. I am the man.

I learned very well the value of patience, the value of not worrying and keeping a strong morale, and becoming something that I was proud of. I had mastered the ability to accept something that people take years and years to master. I could accept the things that were going on. I could accept my situation. I could accept everything and myself and that's something worthy of being proud of, because you couldn't accept me or Mom or the situations that we had to deal with and that's why you left because you couldn't accept.

Dad, I am proud of who I am, and I don't need you. I can take care of my family and I don't need a father figure to come in and take what I have because right now I am the eye of the storm, the impenetrable fortress, the untouchable, the true man that can accept what he has, the everything that fills your nothing.

Dad, you WERE the most honorable person I knew, you used to know what to do in a frantic situation, but now I can, and will fill those shoes. Goodbye Dad, you're nothing to me now.

28

You can aim for the bull's eye every time, but that doesn't mean you'll make it. This became quite clear the day my dad decided to teach me how to shoot the Mini-14 he'd been saving for me.

I impatiently waited for the preacher to end his sermon. I wiggled in my chair and folded my thumbs wanting to go so bad I couldn't stand it. Daddy told me as soon as church was over he'd take me to the gun range. The preacher dismissed us and I half ran out of the church, dragging my dad with me.

My impatience grew stronger as my dad took so long to get everything in the truck. To me it seemed he loaded up everything but the kitchen sink. Though when he finally was ready I was in the car and seat-belted, before he could even blink. I was ready to go! My dad just laughed and jumped into the car.

We drove about thirty minutes out of town until my dad turned on what seemed to be just another red dirt road. We bounced along twisting and turning till we reached an ugly shack and a long, narrow covered area with small wooden tables underneath.

My dad stopped and went inside to pay the fee for me shooting. Once he came out we really just picked a spot to set up our stuff. I held my rifle down waiting for some kind of instructions and I got them. Daddy told me to lay the barrel of the gun of the rest he'd rented from the owner. I gently settled my Mini-14 down into the rest. My dad looked through the scope to aim it toward the target one hundred yards away!

Before actually letting me shoot he showed me how to reload my bullet clip. I shoved five bullets into the clip and I aimed the gun for the bull's eye. I held the butt of the gun in my shoulder. I prepared for the loud noise and the kick from the rifle I knew were coming. I looked into the scope just to make sure and I gently pulled the trigger, bracing myself. I guess the shock of it all was a little more than I could handle, because my shot went much further left than I ever expected it to go. I was in utter dismay as to how I was going to fix it, but I wouldn't give up. I went through fifty rounds trying to get it, but we were running out of bullets quick.

I was on my last five rounds, after this I wouldn't get another shot. I held the rifle in my hands trying not to shake, I stared through the scope aiming dead center on the bull's eye. I thought to myself, "I have to do this! Not only for Daddy, but for me too. Holly, you can do this!"

I looked through the scope one last time and squeezed the trigger. I couldn't see the bullet. Had I really shot so bad I didn't even hit the target? My dad ran to go get the target mat. As it turns out that last round made it within a fourth of an inch from the bull's eye. I was so happy I felt as if I had just done something worthy of a gold medal. I couldn't believe it.

That day I learned how to shoot and I don't know why, but it made me feel stronger. Success comes from trying hard and doing your best. My dad was also happier than a clam. His "Baby Girl" had learned how to shoot.

Dear StepMom,

As a step-parent you may not believe you're an inspiration to me, but you are. You're the perfect role model for teenage girls. Especially for the type like me, bad attitude and a smart mouth. You've taught me how to control my temper when something doesn't always go my way.

"Getting an attitude just makes matters worse," you'd constantly tell me. But most of the time it went in one ear and out the other. "The talk," I'd call it, was always pressuring. No matter what, I'd end up in more trouble than I already was for talking back. "Don't you know that everything starts from home? So if you can't get the basics down at home, you won't be able to keep a decent job in the real world," you explained to me. I'd kept that in mind because I plan to live a joyous life.

Ever since I was eight years old I've dreamed of becoming a singer or a pediatrician, but the road I was headed down led to pure darkness. Containing a poor attitude wouldn't even get me through college. I sat in my room contemplating about how my standpoint influences my future. All the unfavorable conclusions I came upon startled me a bit, so I made up in my mind that I'd make preferable alternatives.

After all of my hard thinking, I decided to come and apologize for all of the wrongful things I've done. Every word that dripped from my lips, into your ear, came from the bottom of my heart. And I meant every bit of it. The tears that were rolling down my burning face were tears of shame. I understood that my actions not only affected me, but everyone around me as well.

Changing a person can lead to changing the world, and that's exactly what happened. When you helped me through it all, it seemed that there was less yelling and more laughter in our household. I appreciate you more and more each day, and I hope you continue to inspire others.

Love always,
Tauequa

Emily Grover – Grade 7 -- Glenn Middle School, San Angelo ISD

I was sitting in a spacious room with an impressive number of plaques and trophies crowding the shelf that ran along the perimeter of the walls. Behind me were about fifteen figures, each protected by a black case and a lock. They all rested on a specially designed wooden rack. Towards the front of me were similar figures, only these were twice as tall with double sized wooden racks. My seat was in second row of chairs carefully placed in a semicircle. It felt wrong to be sitting in this section know as "The Violins" when my brain contained not an ounce of knowledge of this instrument, but I foolishly expected to play it by the end of my first week in middle school. Little did I know that there was a bigger hurdle to get over.

The teacher wore a thin frown and tired, puffy eyes. She took her time to pass out a sketch of a violin with a stick-like thing below it. On her way back to her abnormally tall chair, she took a light brown violin with obviously dark marks of age. She wearily held it up for all to see, and explained each and every part, failing to hide the boredom in her voice. Even so, I listened with intent, being careful not to let my thoughts abandon the subject. It wasn't until she moved on to the stick-like think that my curiosity really sparked.

The moment my ears admitted the word into my brain was when I recognized what it was. I remembered that the bow was the thing that vibrated the strings of a string instrument, thus producing sound. The teacher leaned over and traded the violin for the much newer looking bow. Then she pointed to the long and slender part of the bow that looked like an unnaturally straight branch, and called it the "stick". Next, she moved her finger to a cylindrical metal thing called the "screw", and then to the opposite pointy end called the "lip". From the tip, her finger traveled to the white horse hair, then to the shiny ferrule, which attached the horse hair to a black rectangle with a white dot mysteriously named the "frog." The teacher concluded her lesson of the bow with a very serious statement of how vital it is to memorize the bow's anatomy in order to learn something I would later dread: the bow hold.

The teacher then requested we take out an unsharpened pencil. Although I did not see the connection between an unsharpened pencil and orchestra, I did just as she asked. After the sounds of kids fumbling in their backpacks died down, she asked us to grasp it in our right hand and place all fingers except the thumb on top of the pencil. She then required us to put only the middle and ring finger together, and the other two apart. I was doing just fine until she instructed us to tuck my thumb under the pencil. It was very awkward, and soon my fingers would collapse. This was the dreaded bow hold.

It went on like that for about two weeks: position, tuck, and collapse. Our whole class struggled together, which eventually sucked out all patience from our teacher, thus leading us to lecture after lecture. By about the third week, students started learning the frustrating bow hold. I would end up feeling like the last bird to leave the nest, because I was the only one who had not mastered it. Satisfied with the majority, the teacher moved on without me to string plucking.

A month passed, and the bow hold reared its grotesque head, but I was ready for it. By this time we owned our own bows, so we had to accomplish the task of positioning the bow hold on an actual bow. It was quite saddening—everyone had forgotten how to do it. However, after two attempts, something clicked in my mind, like I had fallen thirty times and just now had on my feet. From that moment and until this very day, I have held the bow correctly with no collapses.

The learning process is not to be rushed, but given time and effort. Learning that bow hold is what makes me the first chair violinist that I am today.

31

Rosalee Guerra – Grade 7 -- Glenn Middle School, San Angelo ISD

To have confidence is to believe. To believe is to know that anything is possible. I was once a person who nobody believed in, but that all changed when I met my very first soccer ball.

"Ahh, Friday is in the air!" I screamed out to the world. "Sure," Sarah said. 'Well, doesn't today feel great?" I questioned as we walked home from school. "Whatever, just remember that next week is the school's sports competition," Sarah said. "Do you always have to ruin my mood!" I complained sadly. Every year there is a sports competition against each grade. The grade that wins in most of the sports gets to have a pool party. This year was the year I promised myself that I would try out for something, but I wasn't good at anything. So I dreaded Monday for the choosing of teams. When I got home, I went straight to my room to think. I thought long and hard, but I still didn't know what to choose, soccer, basketball, volleyball, tennis, or baseball. Soon before I knew it the weekend was over, and Monday morning had arrived. As I got up that morning, I dressed as slow as possible in hope I would be late for school. As I walked to school with Sarah, my mind was still blanker than ever. I only had a couple of minutes to choose as we stood right in front of the school, and said good-bye. I walked down the hallway, and into the classroom, as the bell rang. I went straight to Mrs. Elkin's desk, and said, "Mrs. Elkins, just put me down for any sport, just surprise me." She looked at my long legs, and said, "I know just the one for you." Soon it was time to go outside, so the captain of each sport could choose their team. Suddenly, "Rosie!" the soccer captain shouted my name. I rushed over, and asked, "What?" I thought he needed me, but he really wanted me on the team! As soon as I got home I told my parents that I was on the soccer team, but they didn't believe me. They thought that I had made the tennis team or something different. "Rosie, you would never make it in the soccer world!" my mom laughed. I was angry by then, because I knew I could do it if I tried my best. A week later I had my first practice, it went horrible. Every time the ball was passed to me either it would go between my legs, or my hands would accidentally touch it. Soon before I knew it we had our first game against the sixth graders, and it was a tie. After the game I started practicing even more, and more. Soon I was able to do all sorts of tricks with the ball. One day my mom saw me and said, "Wow, Rosie! That's cool. I didn't know you could do that!" After that everyone could see my improvement. I was so happy that I proved everyone wrong, even myself. Now every year I have been on the soccer team thanks to my fifth grade teacher, Mrs. Elkins, and every year my team always wins.

Till that very day I have been able to do anything if I just believe, and I don't let others stop me from anything.

Bridget Hernandez – Grade 7 -- Glenn Middle School, San Angelo ISD

How do you feel when it comes to learning new things? Maybe you love to try to learn new things or maybe when it comes to try to learn something new you just hate it. Well, to me learning something new in school was easy, but learning to play basketball was a little bit harder. I wasn't the kind of person to try new things right then and there.

I woke up really late on Saturday. I totally forgot that I had to go to a music camp. I started to walk downstairs hoping my mom wouldn't ask why I didn't go to that horrible camp. It wasn't horrible, I just didn't like music. My passion was basketball. I really didn't know how to play and I wanted to try out for the 7th grade basketball team. I love basketball because even if you don't know how to play it's still fun. One day my mom asked, "Why don't you ask your cousin to teach you how to play basketball?" "I don't know," I said. "Why don't I call your cousin," she said. "OK," I said. It wasn't but five minutes and he showed up. "OK, let's start!" he said. So I dribbled, shot, everything I almost knew how to do. "Are you kidding me, practice every Saturday at the gym!" he yelled.

"I hate this!" I yelled. "Why every Saturday, I'm only twelve years old. I should be sleeping!" "Now get up, get dressed, and I'll take you to the gym," my mom said. We got there and my cousin had this angry look on his face. "So, let's start!" I said. "I said 7 a.m. sharp!" he said. "Sorry, we're not at some camp with rules, OK!" I said. He looked at me and said, "Let's start." I dribbled back and forth down the court, I shot till my arms got sore, I ran till I threw up. This went on for a couple of months till I told him, "That's it, I've had it. No more basketball, I did love this sport, but now you made it horrible!" I said. "You told me you wanted to make the 7th grade basketball team, right!" he yelled. "You've been practicing over 3 months now, don't give up!" he said. "Tryouts are next week," I said. "OK, I know you're ready," he said. "Practice is over for today," I said. I went home and fell asleep. The next day at school the Coach said try-outs were tomorrow. I knew I was ready. They had us run a lot, shoot, and dribble. Everything was pretty easy. They said after school the team would be posted. I went to go see after school. I knew if I didn't make it would upset my cousin and me. I looked down the list. I made it! "Wow, I can't wait to tell my cousin," I thought. I went over to his house and told him. I really wanted to thank him. He was tough on me, but it paid off. "I guess when you learn how to do something really well it's from hard work," I said. "Yeah, it is, congratulations on making the team," he said. "Thanks, can't wait for next year," I said. "Get ready, because the practice is going to be harder," he said. "Can't wait!" I said.

"Practice makes perfect!" my cousin says. Those are words from a true leader. I didn't know how to play basketball, but he showed me. I learned to play basketball and to never give up. Now I'm not afraid to try to learn new things, all thanks to my cousin.

Faith is trusting someone to the fullest extent. Faith is closing your eyes and trusting someone to see for you. Faith is believing in the impossible. During a hiking trip in Guadalupe Mtn. National Park, I realized that faith is doing what you can't do alone.

Standing in Bear Canyon, one of the steepest trails in Guadalupe National Park, wind enveloped me. All I could see was wind blowing the trees until their branches touched the ground. All I could hear was the wind whistling through the air. And all I could feel inside myself was fear.

For over an hour my father and I had been descending from the mountaintop. With every step I became weaker, with every blast of wind I grew more tired, and with every stumble I became more and more discouraged. The rocks and pebbles underfoot became pieces of frustration, causing me to slip and fall. It became trickier, and trickier to avoid. As much as I wanted to stop and rest, the wind kept pushing me like an invisible hand. Trudging forward without looking, I ran into my father who had stopped abruptly. I soon realized why. We had come to a part of the trail, where it became so steep it was almost vertical. Tears filled my eyes.

"Dad, I can't do this!" I practically screamed over the wind.

"Yes, you can! Put some faith in me and we <u>will</u> get through this," he responded. He then grabbed my shoulders and looked right into my eyes.

"Do you trust me?" he questioned.

"Y-yes," I responded, though I was still unsure. He grabbed my shaking hands and began to help me descend. His footing was so precise that I never stumbled. His grip on my hand was so firm that I soon lost all fear and began to relax. When we finally reached the bottom of the mountain, I looked into his face and said, "I trust you," and this time I meant it. I trusted him completely.

That day I learned more than just hiking. I learned to have faith. This experience has changed me forever. I now realize that there was more fear inside of me, than there was danger on the trail. Because of my own fear, I learned to put trust and faith in others when I couldn't put it in myself. That is what faith is all about.

David Hubbard- Grade 7 -- Alamo Junior School, Midland ISD

"Ring, Ring, Ring!" The door bell to my grandparents motor home rang I crawled out of the back bedroom bed to go see who it was. But By the time I got there my mom had already barged in with her elephent like stealth. She told me that I needed to hurry and get dressed because the first race startted in half an hour. when I heard that I jumped up and went out side to start inspecting and cleaning my bike.

About 20 minutes later my mom told me to go and put my gear on while she finished cleaning my birt bike and woke up every one.

The next thing I knew I was at the starting line seconds away from the start of the race. The shooter held up his gun and "Bang!" I hammered the throttle but didn't move, my engine had stalled! Finally, slowly but shurely I got going. And every time I went over a jump my engine stalled. 12 laps later I finished in 26th place.

I got back to camp and my dad told me that my engine was stalling because my fuel pump had a slight leak in it and all the pressure leaked out so it wasn't getting fuel to the motor fast enough so every body pitched in and got it fixed.

It was lap 5 of 12 in the 2nd race and I was kickin butt in second place. (a big improvement from the first.) I came around the last turn and saw the checkered flag I finished 2nd and got a trophy.

I was on lap 10 of 12 in the third race and I was on fire! I was in first place leading by a mile takeing jumps and turns like never before. But on the strait away I gained a bit of speed. I hit the table top ramp and cleared it but didn't clear the next jump. I flew at top speed into the next jump "Bam!" My helmet slammed into my handle bars my frount spokes (or frount suspension) snapped sending my shinny new tire soaring over all the people in the crowd the racers raced past me at lightning speed

When I got back to camp my dad took one look at my bike and said "Yep this bike is trash."

"But what about the race, if I don't enter this race then I don't even have a chance at winning."

My dad told me after I got done talking that I could race but I would have to race on my practice bike so thats just what I did.

It was lap 19 of 20 and I could see the finish line. I was in third place so I thought I would step it up a notch. So I hammered the throttle and went ziping by 2nd and 1st place witch put me in first. I rounded the last corner in the season and jumped passed the checkered flag. I did it I won the 12-15 year old division championship. When I got my trophy it hit me at one time ricky carmicheal had won this trophy, and maybe this was the start of my career as a profesional Dirt Bike racer.

35

"Whoah, that's gotta hurt!" We were in Waco at the Heart of Texas Coliseum. I was watching the motocross along with my dad and my best friend Justin. It was January 23, 2006 on Saturday with ten minutes left until the races began. I asked my dad if we could go over to the hat shack and then get something to eat at the concession stands. He said "I don't care just bring me something to eat too." We both asked at the same time, "What do you want?" "I don't know just get me something that looks good, he said.

After we got back with out hats and drinks the races began. The announcer said, "And they're off!" The race started out good the first few laps until there was a fault finding crash. As soon as I looked there were paramedics already over at the scene of the wreck. Everyone was quiet and I saw a few people crying. I could see that some people thought it would be the end of Williamson's career, but I knew it wasn't because I could tell that he had enough strength to keep going, but he was just sitting there. The people next to me were still wondering what happened so they asked me. I said, "You know how he was turning?" "Yeah," they said. Well his back tire slipped and the bike landed on him," I said. Then Justin said, "Look! He's moving; he's moving!" I looked down at the track and saw that he was trying to get back on his bike.

By the end of the race, about the final lap, he caught up to the first place racer. Both of the competitive racers were battling for first and right in front of them sat the finish line. Then the announcer spoke, "Oooooh, so close for the rookie, but not close enough! Williamson lost by a heartbreaker."

Finally, they handed out the awards to the top three racers. "The bronze metal goes to Robert Rivera! The silver metal goes to Josh Williamson! The first place trophy goes to Don Angelo! Congratulations all of you racers and better luck next time!" the announcer said. Then Don said, "Wait! I need Josh Williamson to go to the stand!" Everyone got quiet and listened." For great effort I want to award you the first place trophy. You had confidence throughout the race and never gave up. It takes a true winner to do what you did tonight so here you are and congratulations!" The crowd went wild after Don Angelo's little speech and Josh got the first place trophy.

Searching through the hundreds of "how-to-do" books at the local book store, nothing seemed interesting to me. I was about to give up and go home when a little yellow book caught my eye. It was titled "Juggling for Dummies." Recalling a juggler from a performance in Las Vegas, "Juggling for Dummies seemed to be the perfect book for me.

After reading the book several times on the way home, I made the conclusion that juggling would be easy because it is just a simple pattern of throwing and catching balls. Once home I eagerly tore open the package of balls and began to practice. Unfortunately juggling wasn't a simple pattern of throwing and catching balls as I had thought. I couldn't even perform three throws and catches. Angered, I threw the book and balls on the flore and went to bed.

After eating breakfast the next morning, I walked into my room to find the book staring menacingly at me. It was as if it were challenging me to try juggling again. Accepting the challenge, I continued to practice and actually found juggling to be easier than the previous day. Practicing for what seemed like hours, I was amazed that I could perform up to five throws and catches.

Five more days of practice was extremely helpful because I could now perform up to 15 throws and catches. But unlike the fluid cordination of professional jugglers, my juggling look choppy and uncordinated. The main reason this occurs is because I have to memorize what hand I need to throw or catch with and at what time. Thus if I only know how to make 16 throws, when I have to make my 17th throw I freeze up.

Six more days passed and my juggling was still choppy. In addition, I couldn't perform more than 17 throws and catches. I could try for hours, but I just couldn't do it. Frustrated, I decided to quit juggling.

Several days passed and the urge to pick up the balls and juggle became stronger and stronger. Finally, after a week of not juggling I picked up the balls and started to juggle. From the moment I started I knew that something was different. My arms were cordinated and fluid, barely moving with each throw. And my hands were as light as feathers, catching every ball with ease. I began counting and once I reached 50 I stoped juggling and stood in the middle of my room in awe of what I had just done.

I could not hold in my emotions. Nearly crying, I ran throughout the entire house showing my family my new skill. There were many thoughts dancing in my head, but one thought overpowered the others. I could juggle!

Frustration – the condition or an instance of being frustrated. Frustrate – to cause feelings of discouragement. Frustrated is exactly how I felt one hot, summer day on Brownwood Lake. Frustration was keeping me from my goal of learning to wakeboard.

It was the fourth day of my one week visit to my grandparents' house. Every day I sat on the dock along the shore of the bay, watching large ski boats driving around the lake pulling wake boarders and creating huge waves. I had always thought wakeboarding would be fun, but had never tried it. With nothing to do but fish, and swim with my cousins, I decided I should take a shot at it. I knew my grandpa had a boat and my cousin, Justin, had a brand new wakeboard. Ready to try it, I ran up to the house and asked my grandpa if he could take us out for a spin on the lake. "Sure, I'll take you for a couple of hours," Grandpa had replied. Thanking him, I told him how I wanted to wakeboard, and we went back down to the dock to pull the boat out into the water.

As we drove out into the middle of the lake, I decided to let Justin go first. I knew he had been wakeboarding before and thought I could get a few tips from watching him. Sitting in the back of the boat, I watched Justin closely on what he was doing and thought, "Wow, he makes it look easy. I hope it's as easy as it looks." Crawling back into the boat after about a twenty minute ride, Justin was soaked and told me it was rough out there. I think he saw how nervous I was and told me not to worry. "Nobody gets it on their first try, don't worry, it takes practice. Don't get frustrated either, that will make it harder to learn," he had said. I wish I had listened to him. The first three times I tried, I fell every time, and was already mad at myself. Spitting out disgusting lake water and watching the boat float past me so I could grab the rope, I heard Justin telling me that I was leaning too far forward. Ignoring him because I was frustrated, I grabbed the rope and was ready to try again.

After about twenty tries, I still couldn't get it. It was making me so mad that I couldn't focus. I knew that's what the problem was, but I still didn't try to calm down. I was getting really tired of falling. "If I fall one more time and have to taste that disgusting lake water again, I quit," I said to myself. Sure enough, I took a hard face plant into a huge wave, and got back into the boat. I thought maybe I can get it tomorrow when I'm not so mad at myself.

At seven in the morning, we got up and took the boat out. Justin thought that I should try early in the morning while the water was still smooth. Feeling a lot better, I slipped my feet into the boots on the wakeboard and jumped into the water. After only four tries, I got up on the board and skidded across the lake. I was so proud of myself for getting up. After about two hours of practice, I didn't want to stop. I was having so much fun. I learned not only how to get up, but how to control the board and jump across the wakes. Having a blast, I hated to hear the words, "We have to go back to the house for awhile." I didn't want to stop. I had learned to wakeboard very well. I couldn't wait until we got to come back out.

Staying focused makes accomplishing things a lot easier. Frustration only makes things worse. If you get angry with yourself, just relax for a little while and it will make things so much easier.

The place was absolutely breathtaking. The air smelled crisp, calm, peaceful, and fresh at the same time. The trees were bright and vibrant; it didn't even look real. Then my eyes caught sight of the Maui scene, the falls, and Mount Nolma Falls. It was large and majestic. It gave you the feeling you were insignificant.

I gazed in awe at the twisting trail that led up the mile-high waterfall. I walked along side my mother as the wonderfulness of the place seemed to sink in. Then a bright blue lizard streaked across the path.

Up ahead I spotted an old, winding wilted tree. It had a large gaping hole inside of it. My dad and I hurried ahead to investigate. We peered inside the ancient tree. My dad gasped, "Oh! Do you know what this is? A fox den."

The fox den was messy. Things scattered about, but in a way, it was like art, creative but natural art. We seemed to glide along the beautiful trail for several more minutes. Then, we saw a huge, bulging clump of moss. My mother walked over to it. She said in an excited, wavy voice, "Renee, Jordan, come over here!" Suddenly, she picked me up and set me on the moss. My jaw dropped. The moss felt like a cloud. It was so comfortable. Then, I just lie there, half dreaming, looking up at the sky. It was so overwhelming.

No one talked. My family and I; we just listened. We listened to the birds singing, the crickets chirping, and the breeze rustling the leaves once in a while. I felt as though we were not worthy to speak in the presence of all of this. Then we heard commotion in the bushes. My eyes strained to see what was making the noise. I found it. I saw the cutest creature, a rabbit, big, brown, and fluffy. It had sparkling blue eyes. I inched toward the darling thing. It heard me and in a blink, it was gone.

The silence started once more. We were all quiet. Just eating up the magic around us. We had almost completely walked to the top with out saying a single word, when Jordan exclaimed, "Wow, Look!" We all looked up as if on signal. To meet our eyes was a soaring eagle. He flew with great speed and strength. He glided through the air without a single flap of his wings. We stared at the magical sight for what seemed liked ages.

We began to walk along the trail again, but within a few yards we had already reached the top.

We fawned over the landscape. It was absolutely marvelous. Our eyes trailed from the edge of the land, with the colorful trees and swirling mist, to the end where the huge majestic falls caressed down the smooth cliff. It splashed softly on the rocks and bubbled into the gurgling pond below. Suddenly, the eagle glided down from nowhere and abruptly perched itself on the tree right next to us.

Have you ever been to a World Cup or Super Bowl game? Have you ever seen them on television? If you have, then you would know how good the atheletes are, how high the stakes are, how great the momentum is. Well, with our soccer division, that's how we play. With every move the game could change. As of, I know just how to turn the tide of a one-sided game and pull off a dramatic comeback. Would you, ever, figure that almost everyone can be defeated the same way? Most people, when in the lead, play offense and hope that the other team can't fight back. Well, I am miscellaneous from the people. Foremost, since I play goalie, I wait for the opposition to come, so I can block the shot, amazingly punt the ball down field, and allow our forwards to score.

Likewise, it was the final game of the first day of a tournament. If we are to move on to the next day, we were to either win the game and easily move on or tie the game and the team we faced before loses. The game was long and tiring. Luckily, it was tied at halftime, zero to zero.

At this time we knew that if we were to advance we were going to face our rival and sister team. The team that taunts and mocks us. With their sinister ways, they beat us every time we face them including two championship games! So most of our team panicked. As then, we stepped back onto the field.

The other team kicked off and easily evaded our defenders. Then, shot it, but, I block it. I punted it, they retrieved it, and the race began. The ball went back and forth, up and down the field. Then, the final two minutes counted down.

The other team gained strength and continuously shot the ball. Our defenders tried many times to get the ball. Even if they did get it the opposition would regain it. Then, I decided to use my injured knee as an excuse to rest. So, I used what energy I had to catch a ball that was shot. Then, as soon as, I contact the ball, with a kick, I fall over feinting an injury. The game stops and I lay on the floor regaining energy. Soon after, I get up and I am ready to finish the game.

After then, I take a free kick. An opposing player stops it and it goes into our goal box. I ran back into the goal box just in time to jump up and allow the ball to tip my hand enough to head it away from our goal. But still, it landed inside the goal box. I turned and every player was after it. Then, an adrenaline rush attacked me and I charged for the ball. With amazing speed, power and agility i was just six or seven feet away. Then, I saw an opposing player about to kick it. So, I dive for it. I grabbed it and held it in my hands to recieve a round house kick to my back. The rush left and I heard as the crowd's cheering was as if someone were just a couple inches away screeming as loud as they could in your ear. Soon there after I yelled. Right after I punted the ball, the endgame whistle blew and the cheers got even louder.

In conclusion, if you figure that most people do alot of things the same say, you will know everyone's weakness. Which is how I change the momentum of a horrible one-sided game. But, really the only time I'm at my best is when the other team has great momentum on their side.

What have you learned from this passage? The better you do something is how well you plan ahead, how well you watch other's, and how long you play the game. As for, this can lead to true leadership....

The warm heat from the spotlight covered my face and the only thing I could hear was the sound of hands clapping together. Roses of all colors were landing at my feet and as I bent over to pick one up I heard a gun shot. I woke to find myself in a cold sweat as I leaned over to look at the clock. 5:30 a.m. it read. How could I have been so stupid to not set my alarm the night before? I got up, still in dismay from my dream, and wondered where I had left my dance bag. Irresponsible is what my mother called it, but I simply called it misfortune. "Late again, Miss Lozano?" my instructor said as she raised one eyebrow. "Sorry ma'am. It won't happen again," I assured her. "I hope not," she replied. "From the top." Ever since I was a little girl I wanted to be a prima ballerina and when I turned 6 I finally got my chance to be in ballet. I had always loved to put on my mother's old flat top ballet shoes, but it was different now. Now I dreaded them. They made my feet sore for more than a week at a time and gave me blisters and cuts on many occasions. Every time I mentioned it I always had the question "Do you want to be a prima ballerina?" asked to me.

The slow melody began to play as I gracefully moved my arms and feet. Moving freely like a bird I began to remember my dream and how everyone loved me, except for that single person. I was still in my gaze when the music stopped. "Oh, great," I thought to myself. The only time the music was ever stopped was if I had messed up, but in this case I hadn't messed up at all. I quickly looked at my instructor to see what she was going to criticize me on, but when I looked over I didn't see anger in her eyes. I saw tears. She started to clap her hands faster than I had ever seen anyone able to. She waved for me to sit down in the chair next to hers. She began to tell me in a soft voice, "When you first came to me I knew you would be something great, and when you began to mess up I was hard on you because I knew you could do better. Now my dear, you are the greatest I have taught in many years."

People sometimes criticize you because they know you can do better than what you are putting forth.

"Practice makes perfect." I'm sure you have heard that sometime in your life. Up until one Saturday afternoon, I had never really thought about that truism. That day I learned and experienced what those words mean. It all started one rainy Saturday afternoon…

"I'm bored," I announced to an audience that looked the way that I felt. It had been raining all afternoon and there was nothing to do. Everything on TV was weird or a boring re-run of an ancient sitcom that would never come back. My mom rolled her eyes and told me to pick up a new hobby. "But there's not anything that I like to do," I told her with more patience in my voice than inside myself. She went into her room and came back with a bag made of cloth. Curious to see what was inside, I inched toward her nonchalantly. When I saw what was inside the bag I was horrified.

"No, not knitting!" I practically shrieked. "Only grandmas in rocking chairs knit." I could tell my mom was trying not to roll her eyes or sigh at me. "Look." She showed me a fashion magazine with numerous glamorous stars. Some of them were actually wearing knitted scarves, hats, belts, sweaters, ponchos, and much more! "Well…" I thought about it. My mom knew what that meant and grabbed two gigantic needles from the bag and some pretty bright pink yarn.

She demonstrated how to hold the needles and the yarn. I was getting frustrated. My fingers were either too stiff or too wobbly. They ached and throbbed turning almost red and purple. I didn't want to practice any more. I wanted to learn how to make things like the celebrities wear. I was ready to give up. My mom kept a sly smile on her face every time I would get distraught. After awhile, my frustration turned into annoyance. When I told my mom that I was ready to give up, she encouraged me to try one last time. When I did, it happened, I finally got it! I was ecstatic, showing off to everyone that I could knit! I planned to make everything that I saw in the magazines.

After that day, I was on a knitting hot streak. But I learned something more than the do's and don'ts of knitting. I learned that the old saying really is true. Practice really and truly makes perfect.

As we began, clear, bitter sweat drenched from my fatigued forehead after looking out at the blinding crowd; this afternoon at the classroom Connection Center off Wadley and Garfield was my extensive introduction in the art of theatre and gymnastics. Without the preparation, I would be abandoned of skill and discipline. As you can tell, being part of an act as diverse as this one was arduous to swallow.

In the beginning, about five or six elongate weeks ago, at the very start of summer, I was in an abysmal nap on my maize and beige mixed coloured love seat with my fluffy warm greenish blue tiger comforter all wrapped up and content. Apparently, I was irresponsisble and then lectured on some speech about hypocrisy and trustworthyness. Moments later, I was commanded by my mom to join any program that would keep me awake and hungry to learn (*cough cough* YAY!)

The very next cockcrow, at like 7:00 A.M., I sailed into the metallic silver 2006 Nissan Murano that my family owned to be driven to the YMCA nearly all the way across town and gander on my limited variety of options. The list read: Theatre; golf; big brother/sister program; keep Midland beautiful. Honestly, what do you think I chose?

Eventually, every day during that blistering, firey month, I was practicing with a group of strangers on some play called, "The Arrival of Sam."

At first, I despised giving hardly any elbow grease such as actually participating and enjoying what was ahead of me. But after one ghastly afternoon, a new girl signed up. When my eyes first struck at her long blonde hair, deep blue eyes, cute brown freckles, and thin-compact body, I had to impress her. I am a guy, ya know!

Come next Monday, I was overflawed, but even when sucking at the stunts, I perservered. Then my attitude changed. I fell in love with what I was doing, but still couldn't control what my low-set body was supposed to execute. My timing was just off. When my calls were too early, I'd hold my position, then they were late. I felt immedicable about the grace that was misplaced.

At last, after continuous hours of strain and brief moments of relaxation, I was developing proper technique and motivation. There still was conflict though in the kids. Making friends was almost impossible to the extent where I lost concentration. In unison, the community would laugh when I faulted or overstepped. My other problem was my attitude. The low self-esteem restrained my potential. Without the right frame of mind, I would have a pessimistic point of view, which caused striving pointless.

Weeks later, auditions were held at the triple C and I just knew inside I could dominate the part after my recent ambition. Everything became so natural and obvious to me about where to stand, how to deliver the lines, and what mood to set for the audience. So I gallop onto the stage, emote and enunciate my predetermined lines, and act like I've done this my whole life.

"Wow! Fantastic job!" congratulated the director of this entire event. All the homework was in the bag.

Our director approached the stage and deciphered how hard we worked and what the play was about. To put it in simpler terms, the speech was lame and mushy. I grew fidgety and sensitive to temperature, but I was anxious to be apart of this.

I stared, effortlessly lacking posture at the overpopulated audience and then thought about all I did to be here on the stage. Finally my part came. It was my turn to shine.

As I look back now, I wasn't ever really apart of anything before this. I wanted to lay back and enjoy my days. Now I learned to always perservere, no matter how tough or easy the objective is.

Like my mom always told me, "When in doubt, try, try, and try again."

43

Audrei Meador – Grade 7 -- Herman Furlough Middle School, Terrell ISD

Dear Mom,

    Thank you for always being there for me. Not like being at football games, cheerleading tryouts, church camp, and all of that stuff, but thanks for teaching me a new skill, characteristic, and talent. We were at the annual heritage jubilee and all of the performers were warming up. After stretching we all lined up to show off our tumbling skills. That's when it started. Lauren and Breanna, my rivals were doing back tucks, and the crowd went wild. However, I only did flip-flops.................

    The crowd was amused with Breanna and Lauren's astonishing talent. They would run, skip, round-off, and BAM, there goes a beautiful back tuck. I felt it creeping up my spine. Mr. Jealousy was getting me started. After the performance I was absolutely nauseated. I couldn't stand the fact just because I was a "little nine year old" I wasn't as good as Breanna or Lauren. Now Mom, we both know that I had been doing gymnastics ever since I was 18 months old, but Breanna and Lauren who had been coming for two years already had their back tucks? This couldn't be possible.

    That night I came and sat on your bed. You remember, don't you? Anyways, we talked about the events that had taken place that day, and then….we had a plan. You told me if I wanted it then you would help me. But, I had to put in 110% or it wouldn't work. Every day for five months I trained. I worked on weekends from four to seven, and for two hours on Monday through Friday. I built up my strength, courage, hope, respect, responsibility, faith, and my relationship with you!

    The Fall Show was right around the corner, and I was ready. I just had to do this back tuck. I had to stick it, I just had to. Then it was time. You helped me dress and warm up, then from out of nowhere up walked Breanna and Lauren. They were talking about what tricks were in their routines, and as soon as Breanna said, "Oh, and there's seven backs in mine." I just smiled…………because mine had ten. Well, before I could say a word, it was my time to shine.

    The music blared, the lights shined, and I danced like nobody was watching. I would turn, shake, run, flip-flop, turn around, and for a split second, (right before my first back tuck) you just looked at me, you looked into my eyes. Then you smiled, and nodded your head. I winked at you, looked forward, and ran hard, skipped, round-offed………….and, and BAM, I had done it. I landed it perfectly, and finished my routine with a smile. You came up behind me and said, "Oh, I'm so proud of you. My baby girl has turned into a shining star. And you're better than ever.

    Now I'm thirteen, so that was like four or five years ago, but I still remember the moment that I did my first back tuck. And Mom, that back tuck was just for you. I didn't just learn a new skill, I learned to be courageous, just like you. I love you, Mama.

Love,
Audrei Donn Meador

P.S. I love ya! And I hope I'm still your baby girl, as well as your shining star. I will do my best to keep on shining.

44

Dear Coach Dave,

Hey coach remember when we were at the Terrell Soccer Fields for our first soccer practice?

On our first day of practice the first thing I did was pick the ball up with my hands. And your reaction was to show me the right way to handle a soccer ball. I can already tell you it was going to take a lot more than one time before I got it. I guess it was easier to play when the ball was in my hands instead of on my foot. One day, when you were gone for the whole practice coaching another team, I decided not to touch the ball with my hands at all. I remember being so proud that I ran over to tell you myself.

I wish I could say that was the hardest thing that I had to learn not to do. For some reason my new favorite thing to do was to score for the other team. I mean it almost felt like a habit. But at that age who cares, right? Wrong! Not if you play for the Terrell Roadrunners, and not if you play for Coach Dave. Which is fine by me. But of course you would know that. Thankfully as the season got older I got better. I even scored a few. Even in the right goal.

I remember you asking me if I would like to play goalie this season. Since I liked to use my hands so much I didn't see why I shouldn't. Surprisingly it wasn't as easy as it seemed. I remember every day you would work with me on punting the ball. But the hardest part of the training was learning how to dive. I remember being scared it was going to hurt. But that was the least thing I was worried about. Getting dirty was a really big pet peeve of mine. I could tell it bothered you when I would drop the ball. Finally, all of the diving and punting lessons paid off. When the end of the season rolled around we had won first place in our group. I was so excited when I got my trophy that I remember running up and giving you a great big hug.

After two fun and exciting seasons on the Roadrunners, I began to really love the game. I also learned two valuable lessons. The first one being that you are an awesome coach and two being I wanted to play again. Thanks to you.

Sincerely,
Number Five

Jessica Osborn – Grade 7 -- Teague Junior High School, Teague ISD

"Good morning everyone," said Mr. Jackson over the intercom system. "It's time for the morning announcements. First off the lunch menu is…"

"I don't care about the lunch menu," I thought to myself. "Come on tell us who made cheerleader!"

"Our final announcement this morning is for six lucky sixth graders that made cheerleading! The names are: Page Dillion, Emilee Allison, Brittany Beasley, Allyson Monks, Meagan Venable, and Jessica Osborn."

"Yes, I made it!" I yelled.

"BEEP! BEEP! BEEP!" my alarm clock screamed at me. "Huh?" I thought, I opened my eyes and I was in my bed in my room." I guess it was all a dream." I said it out loud in disappointment. I got up, got dressed, and headed down the stairs to eat breakfast.

"Good morning Jessica," my mom greeted me as I walked into the kitchen.

"Good morning," I replied.

"Are you ready for tryouts after school?"

"Yes, I'm ready but I'm really nervous!"

"Well don't be because you are going to make it. I tried out in the sixth grade and I made it. It was a piece of cake."

"I hope I have the same results."

When I got to school the only thing all the girls were talking about was the tryouts. I guess I'm not the only nervous one, I thought to myself. Each class period flew by and finally the last bell rang and all the girls headed for the gym to start tryouts. When we got there, we drew numbers to see who got to go first. Luckily, I drew number twenty-four so I would have a little time to let my nerves settle down.

Before I knew it, they called my number twenty-three! I was a nervous wreck. "Calm down, it will be okay," I scolded myself.

"Number twenty-four." One of the judges called out.

My heart started to race. I started breathing harder and harder until I was taking in so much air that is started to make me dizzy.

The gym was silent except for the sounds of my sneakers hitting the floor and my heart pounding like a bass drum. I stopped in front of the judges and started my cheer. I was yelling so loud I could hear my voice bouncing off the walls and coming back to me. I smiled my best smile and made my movements sharp. I slapped my hands down by my sides to signal that the cheer was over and smiled at the judges. As I walked out of the gym I couldn't stop smiling.

When the rest of the girls were done we all were called into the gym and lined up against the wall.

"OK girls this was a tough decision. All of you did very well but only twelve of you are going to be a Teague Jr. High cheerleader," one of the three judges announced. "The six lucky seventh graders that will be filling the eighth grade spots are... Brittany Brown, Reagen Mathison, Summer Moore, Casey Winkler, Jesika Allison, and Jessica Foster. Now for the sixth graders. The names are Page Dillion, Emilee Allison, Brittany Beasley, Allyson Monks, Meagan Venable, and Jessica Osborn. The names were followed by whoops and hollers.

"Yes, I made it!" I yelled. I was so proud of myself.

"Were you really nervous?" my mom asked as she walked up behind me.

I just smiled and said, "No, it was a piece of cake."

46

James Patterson- Grade 7 -- Alamo Junior School, Midland ISD

My family loves baseball. We watch every game that comes on. My dad even signed me up for little league and I've been playing every since. One aspect of the game particularly hits home with me: Pitching. I would do anything I could to get on that mound of dirt and hurl a fastball at anyone who challenged me.

When I was younger, although I didn't exactly understand baseball, I watched with awe as the pitcher gracefully goes through his windup, zipping a ninety-nine mile per hour fastball right past the unsuspecting hitter's bat. My dad looked over and asked me, "Son, would you like to learn how to play baseball? We can go get you your own baseball glove, and, in time, sign you up for baseball." I thought, "Well, is the pope Catholic?" and ran off to get my shoes and practically forced my dad out the door. He took me to Big 5, led me to the baseball section, and there I saw my one true love. Sitting there on the cluttered shelf, was a bright red, Louisville Junior baseball glove, just calling my name. We went home and played catch hours at a time, days in a row. All I wanted to do was play baseball.

As I got older, my dad noticed that my soft throw was getting harder, and my hard throw getting harder still. My accuracy was improving, but still not perfect, and I was shaping up to be a pitcher. My dad took me to the local high school pitcher, I pitched for him, he said I was great, and told me to pitch for the Midland Rockhounds pitching coach. I did, and he suggested I go to pitching camp.

Soon I was at pitching camp, and every day after I got back, my dad and I would practice. Finally, baseball season rolled around, and now I could show off my stuff to the coach. The coach, who is one of the most awesome coaches, (besides my dad) I've ever had, and he gave me a chance.

It was game day. The crowds were going crazy, not because of excitement, but because of the extreme heat. Coach called me to the mound in his kind, booming voice. I took a look around, as if I were going to a war I didn't expect to come back from. I slunk to the mound, scared out of my mind that something bad was going to happen. When I finally reached it, the umpire threw me a ball, giving me a few warm-up throws. I took one last look around, seeing the sneer on the batter's face; the toddler in the crowds crying for his mom; my parents, encouraging me, hoping I do well; my coach, smiling; and my team, standing there impatiently, waiting for me to throw the ball. I went through my windup and, "POP". Strike one. I did that enough to strike out two batters, walk one, and force a ground out.

Had it not been for that bright red baseball glove, I could have never reached that day when I pitched my first game. Now I am a pitcher for a Pony League team, and scholarships are in my near future, thanks to my fastball.

47

Bailey Paul – Grade 7 -- Herman Furlough Middle School, Terrell ISD

Dear Momma,

Do you remember that day? "It's a perfect day for riding," you had said. I was nervous and I can still remember the jolt of energy that went through my body the first moment I got up on that horse; the first moment I experienced the love for horses.

I have grown up with horses my whole life. When I was little the only thing my heart desired for was to be a cowgirl and ride horses in the rodeo. You had the same dream for me and you planned on making it come true. Brittany began riding horses in rodeos when she was about ten. At that time I was three and horses were set right in front of me to experience. Riding was in my blood and I couldn't hold back the desire.

The first day I got on a horse was magical. My heart burst with joy showing through my smile. The first feeling of our two souls linking together as we glided gracefully was unforgettable. I didn't know exactly what it was that made my heart so content but when I was on the back of a horse something felt right.

Once I had started I couldn't stop. The horses found a special place in my heart and I vowed to never let go. You were always encouraging me to follow and pursue my dreams. And with horses, the answer was always yes. I kept on riding and our bond became powerful. My childhood dream came true and my love for horses grew bigger everyday. All along the way you were teaching me how to ride and encouraging me to try my best.

The pounding of the horses' hooves thumping the ground in unison with the beat of my heart. The wind blowing my hair wildly. The adrenaline rushing to my head as the pressure becomes unbelievable. I loved it. Rodeo inflicted all of these things on me and competition had come to challenge me. You trained me to Barrel Race and I practiced nonstop. I didn't give up or even let that option slip my mind. I kept pushing to succeed. It was rough, but it made my will to fight for what I wanted stronger than ever.

I practiced and trained to the best of my abilities to finally feel the victory I had been striving for all my life. I wanted to make you proud and show you how your training and encouragement had helped me. All of my hard work and practice paid off. I won ribbons, trophies, and even buckles. I had succeeded for you and the goal I had set many years before had finally been made into reality.

Having horses in my life has proven to me that if I work hard, believe in myself and never give up, I'll be able to accomplish anything I set my mind to. Horses have played a big role in my success and it's amazing how much I love them. Thank you for bringing horses into my life and helping me realize that my smallest dreams can become huge reality in the future.

Love,
Bailey

48

Dear Marcus,

"Ughh!" I screamed. "Why can't I ever beat those idiots with weak monsters and magic cards! I sat in my pine wood desk in my dim lit room, looking at my "Yugioh" cards, my eyes giving way to frustration. I had my deck full of monster cards. That day I'd kill but I could never win. I put my deck back in my purse and decided to go to your house the next day for some advice.

"Hmmm, I can see your point. Well, I've got ten duels today, so here," you said giving me a Yugioh DVD, "It's the first five episodes of the series. You can learn how to duel for real through it."

I popped the DVD of the "Yugioh!" TV series into my DVD player and layed back to enjoy the show. In it, one of the main characters, Joey Wheeler, had the same type of deck as me, no magic, no spells, no traps, just monsters. Joey asked Yugi to tell him what was wrong with his deck. After a while he told Joey the advice that I too, needed to hear.

"Duel monsters is all about combining your monsters with your magic cards. With no magic, heh, heh, heh, your monsters will get creamed every time."   "Believe in the heart of the cards," that was Yugi's motto, and it always came true for him. So, if I trusted my deck, put some magic in it, along with some trap cards to give my opponent a disadvantage, and believed in myself, I could win just like Yugi. I traded, sold, and bought cards online and had the ones I purchased delivered to me. After an hour of switching cards in my deck, I had a full forty cards deck. I called your house and challenged you to a duel, saying that I could do it well, and, in fact, I was a great duelist. You agreed, and said that Shane, your little brother, could be the announcer.

"Duel!" you and I yelled in unison. I was ready to show off my hard work, skills, and faith. You wanted to see if your idea of advice had worked and if that you had made me first string girl duelist in the family.   "The first and only match of the day is Brother faces cousin Stormy!" said Shane, in a big announcer type of voice. "First person's life points to reach zero loses. Each of you start out with four thousand life points. Begin!" The duel went on for fifteen minutes, and at about that time, we both had only a few cards left in our decks, each of us with only one hundred life points left. "I draw," you said, as you drew another card from your deck. "Alright Stormy, it's over. I give up half of my life points so this trap can get the remaining amount of my life points, doubled, from yours."

"Not so fast," I said grinning with pride. "I didn't come this far to be beaten by that. Plus, you forgot about my face down card. I activate it now. It's called "Mystical Reppannel," and it neutralizes your trap card's effect and turns it right back at you. Sorry Marcus, but you lose and I rock."

"Final score, Brother 0, Cousin Stormy, 100. Cousin Stormy wins the duel!!" Shane declared. "How did you do it?" he asked. And we would all later laugh about my answer.

"I believed in the heart of the cards," I replied, with a smirk across my face that would rival even Yugi's.

Craig Rowan– Grade 7 -- Herman Furlough Middle School, Terrell ISD

Dear Mrs. Candler,

It had been a long first day of school and I was tired as I walked into your classroom all sweaty and nasty from gym class. I realized all of your certificates and awards from your past years as a writing teacher. I got real nervous. I thought you were going to be like all my other teachers, cruel and mean. All of my classmates started talking and giggling before the bell rang. I sat down in my desk ready for you to scream at us, but you didn't. Instead you sat down quietly and asked the class to please be quiet. The noise of voices faded away and you began to teach.

About 10 minutes into class you told us to take out a sheet of paper and to write a composition about our favorite memory. I adjusted my sweater and decided that it was going to be a piece of cake. I wrote about the time I went to Medieval Times on a school field trip in my 6th grade year. You told us that we needed to do our best, but the problem was I didn't do my best. I ran into your class the next day, excited to see what I made on my composition. I looked at the board searching for my name. When I finally found it I kind of froze. I made a 2+! I couldn't believe it. I walked up to you mad and frustrated. I asked you why you gave me such a lousy grade. You told me that it was very average and it wasn't interesting. I got real angry and asked you what I could do to make it more interesting. You told me to meet you after school for tutoring and told me to bring a mind with determination to write a real story.

As I walked into the lecture hall, I thought about what was going to happen. I tilted my head to the side and saw that one of the kids was writing a letter. I didn't understand or get why he was writing a letter for a composition paper. When I started to ask him why he was writing a letter, you walked in. You announced that you were going to teach us how to use passion and effort in our writing, using letters.

When tutoring was over I knew how and why I needed to write a passionate story. A couple of weeks later we had an assessment. I wrote a letter to my grandpa who died a couple of years back. I put all of my passion and emotion into the story and all of the work had paid off because I finally had reached my goal and got a 4! Thank you Mrs. Candler!

Your student, Craig Rowan

50

Danielle Rubio- Grade 7 -- Alamo Junior School, Midland ISD

Imagine walking onto a stage to perform for the first time. Your heart is pounding and you feel like your holding a huge amount of weight on your shoulders. This is exactly how I felt when I went to play my violin. I was a small fifth grade girl and I was about to play in my first orchestra concert. At the other end of the auditorium the audience waits patiently for us to play our piece. The conductor gradually walks onto the platform while twinkling lights sparkle down on us. Although this was a moment no little girl could forget, this isn't really where my story begins.

"Everybody please line up to go to the gym," retorted the teacher. We all stood up and walked slowly down the halls and into the gym. It was a completely normal day except we saw a strange looking lady talking to our coach. Hesitantly, we all found our spots in the gym and sat down. Then we waited patiently for someone to introduce us to the woman. She was a tall, slender woman and looked like she was at least twenty years old. The coach finally noticed our confused and awkward faces towards her and so he began to introduce us to the lady next to him. He told us she was an orchestra teacher and was asking if any of us wanted to join her orchestra class. I decided I wanted to try it so after class I told her I was interested.

Days became months and I couldn't stop playing my violin. I became the number one player in her class and step by step I learned how to become a better player. Every time I play the violin I forget my surroundings and focus entirely on the piece I'm playing. That concentration helped me not only in orchestra but I also began to use the concentration I knew I had and used it to study my academic subjects. I usually always would receive high eighties and some occasional nineties and one hundreds on my report card. Once I used my concentration and determination I discovered I had inside of me, my grades in all subjects turned to high nineties to one hundreds on almost every paper I turned in to my teacher.

My orchestra teacher really inspired me to keep playing and to this day I am still playing my violin. Although I have a different teacher, I've been a better student, not only in orchestra, but academically as well. My parents always ask me to play a piece for them and some of my friends ask me how to play a certain part of their music so they can learn how to play it, too. I have come a long way from not even knowing how to hold my instrument to not being able to stop playing my instrument.

With honors and straight A's, orchestra has helped me realize what I am capable of doing and what I'm capable to do in the years to come.

51

Dear Dorthy,

Through the good and bad you stood by me. I know that I wasn't the easiest person to get along with either. You still taught me everything, so that I could be the best there ever was. I know you don't remember any of it anymore, so I'll tell you again for the last time.

That night before I began dreaming I remember my mom tucking me in at night. For the weirdest reason I had an unforgettable dream it was like no others. The next morning I told you all about it and you were even surprised about. I asked you if it was hard to learn how to swim. You told me that no it wasn't.

When I got home that day I told my mother and she just gave me this look. She said, "Now if you're going to do this you are not going to quit, because Rubios are not quitters!" The next day at school I signed up for the swim team.

Tryouts came and I barely made it on the team. The very first practice that I had I sucked really bad. You could tell that the coach really despised me for not knowing how to swim. I knew that if I didn't learn quick I would get kicked off.

After two weeks of practice with you I was one of the best on the team. You taught me everything you knew and I am really grateful for that. Even though sometimes we would argue you still helped me. The next day we had a competition, but when I arrived I didn't see your face. It really upset me, but I still kept my concentration on the trophy. That day I brought home the first place trophy. I looked for you, so that we both could share the glory, me for winning and you for being there to help and guide me.

I went over and asked where you were and my parents said you passed away last night. They didn't tell me this morning, because they wanted me to do my best. I was so upset and furious at the same time. Two weeks went by and I quit. I couldn't take you not being there at practice cheering me on. I knew that you would not accept me doing that, but what you taught me I will never forget and who taught me will never slip my mind either. The type of friendship we had will never be forgetful, because we were like bread and pumpernickel and plus all the things you helped me with will always stay in my heart. All of those things are things that I know how to do very well and always will be because of you.

Your dearest friend,
Xue Consulo Rubio

It's better to have loved and lost than to have never loved at all. Or is it? I find it very hard to believe that someone could love someone enough to have a child with them, but be stupid enough to choose drugs over their child. Well, Michael, a man very unworthy of the title "dad," did exactly that.

I lived in Dallas with my mom, someone I thought was my dad, and my brother and sister. I drove all the way down to San Angelo with my mom to visit my pawpa. We were talking about how I was doing in school, when his phone rang. It was my cousin Calvin.

He asked to talk to me. When we were finished talking he said, "Have your dad call me, okay?"

I replied, "My dad is in Dallas." Then I asked him, "How do you know him?"

He replied, " Michael is my uncle. He is my mom's big brother."

I told him, "He's not my dad." "Ya he is," is all I remember him saying to me.

That's when I asked my mom, "Why is Calvin saying that Michael is my dad?" She looked at me with sorry eyes and said, "That's because he is."

I felt like my heart had been ripped out, and to make matters worse he said, "Yes, I am your dad." I took off running. By the time they caught me I was six blocks away from my Pawpa's house. When I got back I looked at my mom and asked, "Why didn't you tell me?"

Michael answered for her, "because when your mom and I split up I told her that my drugs were more important to me than you were. I still feel the same way." I just walked up and slapped him real hard.

It's been three years now and I'm slowly beginning to forgive him, I try not to think of him. Plus I'm glad he didn't want me because now my mom is married to a wonderful man who I love. I don't mind calling him dad because he has always taken care of me.

53

Boom! Smack! The soccer ball was gliding across the grass. I couldn't keep my eyes off it. My neighbors were playing in their front yard. It looked like so much fun. Then all of a sudden it hit me. I should sign up and give it a go. "Dad! Can I sign up for soccer!" I was yelling excitedly.

Then the next you know I had my first soccer practice. I didn't know what to expect. Would I be good? When I arrived at the soccer fields my coach started working with me. He was showing me how to dribble. Then he said, "You give it a try." So there I was trying to dribble but I couldn't. Every time I touched the ball it went different directions. When I started watching the other kids do it they did it with ease. I knew I was only six at the time but it didn't take me much to realize that I wasn't that great at soccer.

As time went on I started to play in games. That was just a catastrophe. I didn't know what was going on and most of all I was scared of a soccer ball. I was always very timid during the games. After a while my dad started to get aggravated because he was tired of me not doing so well. At that point I was losing all hope. I went up to my coach and told him that I was probally not going to play next year. He looked at and said, "Derek, I know how hard soccer is for you right now but as time goes on you will get better." That sure boosted my confidence up and from there I decided that I wasn't going to give up.

The next year I signed up once again. This year I told myself that I was going to improve. At practices I was learning how to dribble and finally I started to get the hang of it. I could actually touch the ball and it would go where ever I wanted it. I knew it was going to be a better year. Then that following Saturday I still remember til this day I scored my very first goal in a game. I was so happy I couldn't think straight. That game changed me. I felt like I was on top of the world. From then on out I wanted to go to soccer practice. I wanted to learn and get better. At every practice I was showing improvement. When it came to dribbling a soccer ball down the field I was going to be the best. I kept that mentality in my head and you know what, it was coming true. I started to be able to dribble at a high speed and every once and a while put in a little move to beat a defender. My passing was always superb and I always passed the ball. That is what made me a good player is passing the ball and being smart. Thanks to the soccer practices I started to become a key player on my team.

The next season I became a threat to other soccer teams. In games I would score at least a goal and I would have a few assists. That season my team won first place in our league. Everybody on my team would count on me to step up for the team and score a goal or set one up. I was becoming the playmaker but I knew I still could always make some improvement.

After my Rec seasons were over I tried out for West Texas United Soccer Club. A soccer club picks the best players in a town to travel and play other club teams. I have also managed to actually get to practice and play with the Texas state team. I have transformed as a soccer player and can play it well. I'm overjoyed that I learned how to play it and been so successful while playing. Hopefully one day it could be my career.

Valerie Sanchez -- Grade 7 -- Alamo Junior School, Midland ISD

The sun was burning at ninety-nine degrees. There was no wind flowing. I needed a cool breeze to calm my nerves down to ride that two-wheeled monstrosity!

"Go on! Ride it!" My older sister, Gaby, commanded impatiently. "I know! But it's too hard to balance on!" I replied putting one wheel over the seat. The bike was shaking as I tried to balance. Gaby sighed and put bothe hands on the seat. "I'll push you and then you can go. I looked frightened! But I managed to shake my head up and down. "Alright then! Here we go!" And off I went holding on very tightly to the handle bars.

The bike's front wheel was turning left to right! I didn't know how to control it! Finally I lost it. I could smell the dry, yellow, grass against my cheek. My sister called out, "Hey, are you ok!? You fell pretty hard!" Then I felt her hand lift me up to my feet. I had tears forming in her eyes. "Don't be a baby! I learned how to ride a bike without training wheels when I was eight!" I didn't reply to my sisters comment, I was way beneath angry. She glared at me and stomped into the house.

I stared at the bike for a moment. Then I picked it up and put my leg over it once more. I thought, "I have to do this! I have to! I can't just let all this time go to waste." It would have been intolerable to give up now.

One foot was inplanted to the ground, so I used that as a small boost by kicking the ground. The bike was moving slowly but when I was peddling it moved faster and faster! I held the handle bars firm and steady. I smirked. After riding for a couple of minutes I accomplished riding a two-wheeler bike! Not four wheels two!

I called out for Gaby outside. She finally looked out of the house with a bored face. "What?" she asked. "Look I learned how to do! Watch!" I then performed one leg over the seat a kick to ground and top it off, I sped off on the bike! "You did it! Wow! Look at you ride! Great job!" my sister congraduated.

The sun was steaming hot but a fresh, cool breeze rolled my way as I was riding the magnificant, two-wheeled, bike with such ease! Plus to hear my sister giving me compliments also gave a high rise to me! Ahh. The fresh breeze of a job well done never felt so good.

As I sit and begin to contemplate various things, I start to think of my cooking familiarities. I come from a line of relatives that are known to the arts of cooking. My grandma and grandpa used to own a restaurant that was famous not only for its astonishing atmosphere, but for the fresh vegetables served with every meal. With every bite you had a new feeling of the restaurant. Before I began to learn to cook, my grandma pulled me aside and said, "Baby, when you cook let your life be enhanced with the love of cooking, don't ever cook if you're not going to put your heart and soul into it." I remember it as if it was yesterday. My grandma passed away exactly one week after she said that to me, and I will always hold those words in my heart. My cooking aspiration rocketed after she said those words to me.

I enjoy cooking because most of the stuff I cook inspires me. My biggest inspiration food is Jamaican recipes. When I cook Jamaican recipes, I think of it as if I'm back in Jamaica running wild and cherishing the great opportunity that was bestowed upon me. I like who I am and where I come from because the love I have for people is incredible.

When my grandma passed she left me with a book of her homemade Jamaican recipes. I decided to add on to it. My recipe is called Kum Ya Li Yun Ti. I use a blend of Jamaican spices and a bunch of home grown herbs. I use all kinds of Jamaican spices, but my favorite is one my grandma made up called Kum Yali Baba Tambe. My favorite herbs would have to be basil and mint. They give me a feeling of home when I taste mint in it. This makes me think of the ocean and dolphins swimming around free and singing to the sound of the wind. Basil makes me think of a romantic candle light dinner next to the Caribbean Sea listening to the ocean.

I live day by day not worrying about tomorrow or three weeks from now. I live and take things into consideration that is what I do well.

Alissa Skinner -- Grade 7 -- Herman Furlough Middle School, Terrell ISD

Dear Mrs. Candler,

     I remember sitting in the back of your room not willing to work or make an effort to do anything. But I wasn't the only one everyone was lazy. Nobody wanted to do nothing. I mean all these compositions you had us doing. We just wasn't feeling it. We had a composition every week and they were hard to get done because of all the basketball games and all the extra stuff we had to do. Yeah I know school comes first but you was killing us. Then you asked for the composition that we started on last week that was due that day. So everyone was passing their papers up. When you got all of them we could tell you was mad. Because either people did not do it or they didn't finish. And the ones that were finished were crappy. You looked at the papers then looked at us. Then you threw them down and said, "This is crap. You want to give up on yourself because you don't know what to write about or you're tired. Please, y'all, the TAKS is next week. And I don't know whether to keep trying or give up. Y'all are really killing yourself." Then all the sudden a tear hits the floor and then many more. Your face appears red. And all the rage was gone and turned into sorrowful defeated Mrs. Candler. Some people thought it was funny. But I knew that it was not funny hurting someone. And there was nothing funny making you feel like you did not do your job. Also there was nothing funny about you saying that your regular and special ed kids are doing way better that your sixth period a.m. class. I felt so bad. I felt as if I was killing you. See you put all your faith and time to teach us to become wonderful writers and this is what we do. So I knew what needed to be done. I talked to some of my friends and we all decided that we was going to do better and work hard. Because we knew that you taught us well and that you loved us and cared about us. A week passes and here we are again turning in our papers then we get the results back and…we did it we made threes and fours. And we couldn't of did it without you. You taught us to believe in ourself and have faith. You taught us to write well and not to let your pen control you, you control the pen. I learned a lot from you and now I write well. Because at first it was like pen and paper were enemies now because of you they're friends. I want to thank you for having faith and not giving up on us. And that's just how much you care. And how much I love you.

Have you ever judged someone by their looks? We all have, and well…ninety-nine percent of the time, what we think is wrong. You've probably walked by someone and think, "Oh, she looks mean and snooty. I would never hang out with her!" But probably on the inside, she was nice and sweet and a wonderful person to hang out with. So, one thing I've learned to do well is to NEVER judge someone by their looks.

Judging someone by their looks can be bad, rude, or just plain old mean. Believe me; I've learned the hard way. Last year at my old school, there was a new girl who just moved from Puerto Rico and her name was Shadanno-Linh. She had a very funny accent (or at least that's what I thought at the time) and her clothes looked old and torn-up as well, a little bit too big for her. She was very puny and her hair looked messy and greasy. Since I was judging her by her looks, she looked mean and nasty.

Every time she would walk close to me, I would step away from her. When I was with my friends, I would always say mean things about her and I would never let her hang out with us. Little did I know, one of my friends, Katleign, was related to her! So after she heard the mean things I said about Shadanno-Linh, she got angry at me, and so did the rest of my friends (since they knew a lot about her). They all stopped talking to me and they started to give me these mean and grave looks every time I tried to talk to them. I had lost many of my friends, and the way they treated me made me know how Shadanno-Linh probably felt when I did these mean things to her.

After about a week or so, I decided to call Katleign and apologize to her, my friends, and especially to Shadonna-Linh. They all forgave me and so I decided that we should all get together and have a slumber party. So on a Friday night, my friends and I all went to Katleign's house and Shadonna-Linh was there! I started to talk to her and I learned that the reason she moved to Louisiana was because she had no place to live because her parents had been shot dead by two drunk teenage boys. I also learned that she wasn't as fortunate as most people were and that before her parents had died, they lived behind an abandoned store in the back packing lot.

Shadonna-Linh died on December 24, 2005, at the age of 12 from cancer. She will be forever remembered by me as the sweetest person ever.

I've never felt a pang of guilt like this before. I definitely learned my lesson to never judge someone by their looks. The reason Shadonna-Lihn looked like she did was because of her cancer. But I now understand that it doesn't matter what you look like on the outside, because inside…Shadonna-Linh was the most caring and sweetest person ever.

Aramis Torry – Grade 7 -- Glenn Middle School, San Angelo ISD

Always try your best, and you will be rewarded. It doesn't matter if you win or lose. The only thing that matters is that you tried your best. You don't have to be in a contest or a race. You will still be rewarded by the feeling you get of accomplishment. If you work hard and try your best, you will always win. You will win satisfaction.

I was seven years old, practicing my staff form for the tournament in Snyder, Texas that was coming up. I had to get my form just right, and I couldn't make any mistakes.

"Oh, I'll never get this right!" I complained to my instructor when I dropped the staff again. "This is too complicated!"

"Just keep on trying. You'll get it right, and there's still plenty of time before the tournament," said my instructor patiently.

"It has to be perfect though!" I said aggravated.

I kept on trying to master my staff form with no mistakes, but I was having bad luck. I was either forgetting a step, dropping my staff, or adding extra stops. I began to get annoyed with my form and decided to take a break.

I stared around the do jong, which was the work out room, thinking about my form. I closed my eyes and concentrated.

"I can do this. I can master my staff form. It's easy, and I still have plenty of time," I told myself.

I got up from the floor and decided to try my form again. I stood at the beginning stance and started to do my form. I then opened my eyes and looked at my instructor. His face was still, and he stood there motionless.

I looked at his face getting scared.

"What did I do? Did I do something wrong?" I asked him nervously.

He stood there still motionless, and finally a smile started taking over his face.

"You did it! You mastered your form!" he chuckled.

"I did it! I finally did my form right!" I said in astonishment.

"Yes, you did it!" my instructor cheered.

I felt so excited. I finally mastered my form I was working so hard on. I couldn't believe I could finally do my staff form without one single mistake. I started cheering and jumping up and down.

"Mom! I can finally do my staff form without a mistake!" I yelled as I rushed to her excitedly.

"I can't believe it! You finally did it! You're going to do great when you go to the tournament!" my mom exclaimed.

We all cheered together excitedly at my accomplishment. I just felt so joyful at what I had done. It felt so good to know that I had succeeded in mastering something I had worked so hard at. At that moment a rush of pride swelled up inside of me, and I just stood there, feeling a great amount of satisfaction.

Always try your best, and you will be rewarded. To master even the smallest things takes time. You just need to be patient and try your best. Even if you don't win, or if you're not in a contest or a race, you will still win satisfaction. The only thing that matters is that you tried your best. If you work hard, be patient, and are determined, you will always reach your goal. Your goal can be big or small. The only thing that matters is you tried your best.

59

One thing I learned to do well is how to be a good friend and not judge people. All my life I've been a sweet girl who was hardly ever mean to people. I'd help friends when they were in need. If I saw someone I didn't know who needed help I'd still help them. Whether I knew them or not, I was always nice. But this year all that changed.

Everyday in the halls of Alamo Junior High I see someone getting bullied. When I witness this happening, it makes me think about how I treat people. A few months ago I wasn't as nice as I am today. I guess I was just trying to fit in, and felt like I had to be mean to innocent kids. As my friends and I would walk down the hallway and see kids being shoved around by other kids who think they're the boss of everybody, we'd just laugh and keep walking. Or if we saw someone in the middle of the hall on their hands and knees trying to pick up their fallen papers, we'd just continue walking. We'd also judge people by the way they dressed or how they looked. Everyone else judged people; why couldn't we?

Then one day I made a rude remark to my friend, Brianna, and she called me something I never want to be called again. Once I heard that, I froze with my mouth opened in shock I thought about how much I had changed. Do you know how many feelings I probably hurt? I surely don't. What happened to the sweet girl I used to be? Peer pressure overcame me and turned me into something I'm not.

So now when I see kids getting bullied in the hallway, I don't laugh and continue walking. I do what's right and see if that person is okay. My friends and I don't judge people anymore. We realized that we should be nice because nobody is perfect. Even though somebody doesn't have nice clothes, they could still be a good person underneath. But you wouldn't know that unless you talk to them and become their friend. When I find myself starting to be mean to someone, I stop and think about the golden rule. "Treat others the way you'd like to be treated." If everyone followed that rule, the world would be a better place.

After I look back at how I used to treat people, it makes me even more determined to be nicer. I don't ever want to change into somebody I'm not. The golden rule is a rule I abide by every day. It helps me to be a better person, and I'm thankful for that.

Yvette Villanueva – Grade 7 -- Herman Furlough Middle School, Terrell ISD

Dear Grandpa,

Nearly 4 years have passed since you taught me a new skill and I couldn't thank you more. I can still remember myself sitting in front of the T.V. trying but failing to learn guitar. I was ready to give up but you helped me and told me to keep trying and I remember every detail of those two months.

It was Christmas day and I couldn't wait to open my gifts as any child would. As I opened my gift from my parents, I could believe my eyes. I had gotten a cherry-red electric guitar! It was something I had always wantd and dreamed of playing just like the people on T.V. so I was extatic. This was something I really wanted to learn how to play.

Once we came back to our house in Terrell, I began to learn guitar nonstop for at least two weeks. I bought countless book and DVDs on how to play guitar but none of them seemed to work. I even asked my parents and anybody who would listen to help me learn but nobody had the time so I began to play guitar less and less until finally I quit trying to learn how to play all together. I didn't want to quit playing guitar because I really hoped it wouldn't end up like everything else I've ever tried so there was still hope in my mind. I was really struggling but I didn't once think of asking help from the one person who my parents had told me about several times before that knew how to play guitar. You, Grandpa.

Two weeks after I stopped playing guitar, you came over to our house after coming back from Mexico. The first thing you did after saying "hello" to everybody was come into my room and check in on me. And, seeing as you love guitars, you noticed the guitar the second you walked through the door. I remember every word you said to me about it. "Wow! That's a nice guitar you got there. Do you know any songs on it? What about chords? Do you want me to teach you how to play it?" At that last remark, I smiled and told you, "If you had asked me that 3 weeks earlier, I would of probably said, yes. You can have the guitar if you want it." When I told you that, I could of sworn that I saw you smile and a gleam of happiness passed through your eye because you wanted the guitar but it disappeared as quickly as it came so instead you insisted that you teach me and I accepted.

With your help, I quickly learned how to play my guitar. You came over everyday and sat next to me for at least 4 hours each day until I learned how to play at least 4 or 5 songs. I was beginning to think that if I practiced with you, I would learn a lot better than with someone else because through the whole thing, you never once yelled at me or said something mean which made learning a whole lot easier. I was really happy learning with you and I thought this would last a long time.

But learning with you didn't last long because around a month later, I received news that you had passed away in your sleep. I was saddened by this news and I stopped playing the guitar for a while because it reminded me too much about the time we had spent together. But then I thought of something. You worked so hard to teach me guitar and spent so much time so why should I stop? Then it would have all been for nothing. This made sense so I went back to my guitar and used you as my motivation to keep playing and learning. I practiced morning noon, and night for one whole year without giving myself a day off, I kept at it until I got to be as good as you were. All I did was keep you in my thoughts and practice as much as I could.

I am sad that you passed away but with your help and memories, I learned to play as well as you and that's something that I will always remember. Rest In Peace Grandpa!

Love,
Yvette

61

The Antic Spring

Have you ever remembered an event only because it was a struggle? I get frustrated very easily during struggles, but a lot of the struggles I've been through have been some of the biggest learning experiences, funniest times, and favorite memories I have had.

About six weeks into the school year, the seventh and eight grade drama teacher had just assigned the parts for the one act play The Antic Spring. The scripts had been sent all the way from New York City a few weeks before. I have read very few plays through out my life time, but the one act play my teacher had decided for the drama class to perform was by far the stupidest play I have every read! The play was set in the fifties, and it was about a picnic that was completely planned out by my boring character that turned in to a horrible day. Personally, I would have preferred a more felicitous and modern play, and I am positive everyone in drama would have (at the time) too. After everyone had finished reading through the scripts several times, we went to the stage that was in the auditorium. The temperature in the auditorium was extremely hot. Even if you only walked around on the stage for a few minutes, you would feel over heated! Surprisingly, I could handle the boring part I had received, the temperature in the auditorium, and the stupidity of the play, but my ability to optimistically handle everything didn't last long.

Mrs. Hunt, the drama teacher had never taught a drama class before, so because of this inconvenience, she decided to have an assistant drama teacher. Kyle, a senior in high school, became the assistant, but he acted like he was the actual teacher. Kyle treated Wade, a cast member, better than anyone else, even though Wade had the worst attitude, no ability to listen, and the most annoying personality! The most annoying things about Wade were his habits. He thought it was funny to shock people! Wade shocked me repeatedly, and I finally had had enough. I told Kyle what Wade did and he told me Wade wouldn't shock me if I were nicer to him. I was nice! Then Kyle made the cast members get in a circle with Wade in the middle and hug Wade! After we sat down Kyle told everyone to be considerate of Wade. He started this big lecture about how we could learn from Wade's good attitude. Wade never had a good attitude, and he will never have one. Kyle also told us that we may hate him now, but we would love him after we went to competition and won a place! He told us that wade 'WOULD" get best actor, and the other cast members "MIGHT" get some award! I had had enough! I considered quitting drama, but I felt that I couldn't let the other cast members down. The other cast members wanted to quit as bad as I did. We even made a plan to not have our lines memorized by the deadline so we would get kicked out, but we never put that plan into action.

Before I knew it the competition was two days away! I went with the other cast members to Centerville for a practice run. I performed the worst I had every done and so did the other cast members! We didn't worry about it because we couldn't do anything about it except practice. The next day, we did so much better! We actually got third place! Kyle was right about one thing, we hated him at the beginning, but we love him now!

I am really glad that Kyle helped us because I don't think we would have got a place if he hadn't. The cast members and I shouldn't have worried about Kyle's crazy opinion because there is no point in worrying about something you can't change. If someone who is older than you is helping your teacher, and they are really annoying, you just have to grin and bear it because you have to respect your elders even if they are disrespectful to other people. It's really satisfying seeing something you struggled through, but you stuck with it and kept trying. I, along with the other cast members were really happy after all of this happened, and I know that it's one memory I'm never going to forget.

I walked into a large room and looked around, concerned why we were here. My grandma took my hand and led me to a window overlooking many babies. Each baby was in a crib. Cords ran along to machines and some even went inside a baby! As we walked into another room I asked, "Where is Katelynn?" When my grandma didn't answer I looked up and saw tears in her eyes. I immediately wanted to leave.

She took my hand with a sly smile on her face and we walked through double doors. A nurse handed us both a suit, shoes, and mask. My suit was very big on me and the shoes kept falling off. The only thing that fit was the mask.

The nurse led us into the room with all the babies and carefully arrived at a crib with a tiny baby inside. I was very confused on why we had stopped here until my grandma explained it was Katelynn. It didn't look like Katelynn to me. She had cords running into her neck and under her nose. The nurse explained to me that my little baby cousin was ill. She called her a "Miracle Baby." I couldn't even touch her because it might spread germs and make her worse. We went into the waiting room until my family arrived. I asked my mom what was wrong with Katelynn and she sadly replied, "She is a premature baby." She explained that Katelynn had been born early, and needs help to survive.

The next day I went to school and collected money for Katelynn. I earned twenty dollars, thinking that I was a hero. I skipped into the kitchen with a smile on my face and anxiety to tell my mom. She walked in crying and carefully explained to me that Katelynn hadn't survived through the night. I burst into tears and ran to my room. I cried for hours hoping that this was all a dream. My mom came in and comforted me. She said that tough things happen in life and we had to stay strong. I had just lost my best friend and all the dreams of us playing dolls and having tea parties were gone. I took the money I had to the Miracle Network for other children in honor of Katelynn. I'm strong now and try to help other children the best I can.

Katelynn was a strong baby and even though I only saw her once I knew she was special. Some people don't even get a chance to live, if you do then take it. Live for those who don't get to and help other children like Katelynn.

Danny Aguirre – High school – Lee High School, North East ISD

A friend who could talk you into doing something you know you should not do was not a friend at all; that's at least what I thought. That's why I did not get in the car with him that night. That night he had been drinking a lot. So when he told me to get in the car I was automatically thinking "no," but knowing he was my only ride home made me think about it. That's when he turned around and I looked at his eyes, they were crimson red, and his blinks were slow and lazy, one eye looked at me while the other one drifted off into the night sky. If it wasn't for the car that he was leaning on he would not of been standing. After taking that long look at what I thought was my friend, the words mumbled out of my mouth, "No." "What," he asked angrily. "I'll walk, man, don't worry about it," I said. "Listen, man, I'm your only ride home," he stuttered. "I said don't worry about it," I told him. And without answer or comments, he turned around, got in the car, put it in drive, and drove off. I stood there wondering if I had made the right decision, but then I looked at those taillights and they reminded me of his eyes, those bloodshot eyes. I turned around and began my journey home. Halfway home I thought about him, I wondered if he got home all right, then I wondered if he had swerved off the road, hit a light post, and was now lying in a pool of his own blood. But I did not want to think about it, so I walked faster, then I pictured his funeral, in a church, everyone dressed in black and his mother lying on the coffin crying and screaming while his father with tears in his eyes tries to pull her off. Those thoughts brought tears to my eyes, and I was now running. As I rounded a corner of the street, my heart sank. Farther down the street there was another turn I could see blue and red lights with smoke drifting off into the sky. With tears streaking down my cheeks I ran to the turn as quickly as I could, all the while those visions kept replaying over and over in my head. When I got to the turn my heart was now completely gone. I saw his car totaled and a street lamp at a 45° angle, his windshield shattered. I then saw a pool of blood, the fear and sadness overtook me as I took a couple of steps back. Two police officers stared at me, they did not know what to say, neither did I. An ambulance took off, I knew he was in there, I knew he was dead. Then I remembered our last conversation. I sat down, the vision of his funeral played one last time in my head. I made a choice…now I gotta live with it.

Memory is a strange thing, any smell or sound or even taste can bring memories of old places back. Sometimes they are bad memories like when a war veteran hears a loud noise and thinks it's gunfire, but sometimes the memory helps you feel connected to a certain place. For example when I was younger my grandfather used to smoke his tobacco pipe in a big recliner that sat in his living room, and every time we went to visit, the house smelled of the sweet vanilla aroma that the smoke carried. While sitting in that room, I learned a lot from him. In between puffs he taught me about the war, old movies, even how to fix cars. I always loved going to visit and hear about some cool trick to make engine rattle stop, it was this type of conversation that gave me the warm sense of everything being in order with the world.

Now I'm older and my grandfather has passed away, but the memory of sitting down in front of his chair to hear stories come rushing back to me every time I smell that tobacco. My grandmother feels the same way so every year on his birthday she gets out the old pipe and lights it a little bit to bring back that sweet smell of the house my grandfather built which is so special to everyone in the family. Memories like my grandfather helps us stay connected to the house in a special way and I'm glad we have such a positive memory attached to it.

I realized now how hard some bosses have it. I'd always thought this moment would be of giddy enjoyment, with the pleasure of savoring the words in my mouth as my face flared with flame, surrounding a hideously wide grin. To watch the person sink back, fall to my knees, to cry and sob and beg me to take them back. That they cannot go on with life without this job. Cartoons always had it that way. And so since I was what five? Since then, I'd always wanted to be the macho man firing the nerd.

Then again, this what was happening now in reality, was complicated. This was agreeing in the beginning to something I was never quite sure of, I'd jumped into it because it was offered and seemed like an opportunity. That was three months ago.

Since then, I have been insulted, bathed in sarcasm, shattered my ego from a million to one, felt desperate, useless, untalented, the whole lot. I had slaved over my passion, perfecting it for a man who brushed it aside with one unsatisfied look at me. Our next appointment was three days away, and I grew desperate. Either go or quit. That's when I decided; I'm firing my private lessons teacher.

Actually, I'd sat there at lunch bitterly complaining about it, how I had to learn 'The Firebird Suite' in three different keys in seventy-two hours. That was when Scaie slammed her bottle of Coke down.

"You, you bickering child, pull yourself together!" she snapped at me, cramming an Oreo into her mouth. I watched her cheeks puff out with the presence of food and couldn't tear my eyes away. "You…I mean, this needs to stop," she seemed to collect herself. "If you hate him that much, fire him."

My eyes snapped up from their locked position. "I can't fire," my eyebrows raised- "I can! I shall fire him! But…" my voice trailed off, weighing the options that had the force to resink the poor Titanic, iceberg in its side and all "How?"

And so she plunged. Now let me admit to you, she is quite a speechmaker, I found my hopelessness fail me and my mind grinding away, forming plots. Scaie told me of her past horrid teachers. Like the one that told her to go find a sleeping baby. Watch it breathe, and try to imitate it. She left him within the next week. Of another that lost himself in his own stories of tribes than ate raw horse guts, which pertained in no way to the clarinet and its music making. How all she had to burst into tears in front of her mom when her very last instructor ended his final lesson with "I've seen more peas in a peapod than I've seen music from your horn." And he'd said it with a straight face.

A flame of courage burst within me and I leaned over and snatched up one of Scaie's last Oreos. The hope of saving my musical soul was back, and I ran to the bathroom to call my mom. The entire walk to the potty, all I could think of was, "What do I say, what do I say?" I got there, hid in a stall and dialed the number. The moment I heard my mother's anxious voice was the moment I burst into sobs. I half wanted them, half meant them, but soon I fought it down and told her my hate for my teacher. I guessed the shock of it was what made her agree so hastily, and she said if may call him myself to discuss this. So I did. My heartbeat grew rapid as I heard the rings.

Then, "Hello?" It was he, and I knew he saw my name on his caller ID. I decided to make it short.

"Hi Mr. Duoin? You're fired." I snapped the phone shut and breathed in the sweet air of freedom.

Paul Bradshaw – High school – Hall Academy – Aldine ISD

I guess I didn't know what to do. I really didn't. I watched as people would get jumped left and right. I watched as drug deals went down. I watch as my best friends got arrested and taken away for a good nine to ten months. I didn't know what I wanted to do with my life. I rally didn't. I didn't even know where I was headed. I saw everything that I was doing at that moment in time and I felt as though that was good enough. As if I couldn't change what I was doing. I didn't care. The people I hung out with were cool to me, and even though they did everything that society frowns upon, I still considered them good people. I sat there and started at Danny's face bleeding. His blonde hair glistened in the light that reflected off the moon. I couldn't believe that he was hurt. Nick was my friend and I didn't understand what had just happened. One second, we were all friends, and then another second, Brad was all over him. Just pounding away. He then pulled him outside to his own back yard and stabbed him. Reality didn't hit me until Arthur slammed my back against the wall.

He was just screaming, as if the whole thing was my fault. He wanted to know what happened. I didn't know, so I really didn't know why he was asking me. Arthur was all older than us. He was like the parent of the group, he knew where everything was going to go. He knew that Danny and Mac would be in prison at one point in life. He knew that Rick would probably crash his car because he drives so crazy. He also knew that I didn't belong with these people. He knew that I wasn't the little rebel that the rest of them had been when they were my age. He knew that I was doing good in school and that I didn't need to mess it up, but honestly, I didn't know that and I really didn't care. Brad started dragging me across the yard and put me in his truck. The ambulance was turning the corner as he started up the truck. He turned on Aldine Westfield and drove straight. He didn't say anything to me. The radio wasn't on. It was just silence. I could hear the wind hit the car at 45 miles an hour and then leave us to hit the car behind us, but I couldn't hear anything else.

When we got to my house, jonathan stopped the car and put it in park. I looked around as if I actually knew what was going on. The only thing I remember him saying to me was, "Stay home tomorrow, Paul. Just stay home.

I didn't know what he was trying to say until I got in bed that night. I realized that I was falling in with the wrong crowd and it really didn't make much sense. Of course I wanted to have fun, but I didn't want to ruin the rest of my life in the process. I realized that there was so much more to life and that I need to embrace that the next day, I stayed home. I took care of my neice for my sister and brother in law and I started talking to my parents again. A week later, I saw Arthur in my neighborhood. He looked at me for a good twenty five seconds before telling me that Danny had died and that Brad was dead as well. He said that he wanted me out of that scene. Even I wanted me out of that scene, really. I told him how much what he said the other day meant to me and how I was planning on staying in school and doing everything right. That was the last time I saw anyone from that group again. It was like they all dissappeard after awhile. I look back on it now and I realize that what Arthur said made me keep my life in order. I thank him for that.

AOL Instant Messenger Conversation

Bubbajoe699: Hey, Tony!

Dimeatone13: Fred, what's up, dog?

Bubbajoe699: Nothing much right now at the moment. How about you

Dimeatone13: Nothing much here either. So what are you doing later today and tonight?

Bubbajoe699: I'm probably going to go over to Casey's house then we were planning on going over to the evil lady's house, Galenda, and were going to toilet paper her home!

Dimeatone13: What?

Bubbajoe699: Were going to toilet paper the evil witch ladies house!

Dimeatone13: When, tonight?

Bubbajoe699: Late, around eleven o'clock or a little later. When else?!

Dimeatone13: Oh, I don't know. My head is up in the clouds right now, so excuse my slowness.

Bubbajoe699: So d you want to tag along?

Dimeatone13: Ummm … well, actually I don't think that I should. Actually, you probably shouldn't go there. It doesn't seem like such a good idea. You have heard the stories. She might -

Bubbajoe699: What? Are you chickening out on me? Chicken, Chicken, Chicken! Why don't you want to come along, nothing bad is going to happen.

Dimeatone13: I just have a bad feeling about doing this.

Bubbajoe699: Oh, sure, You've gone and told on Casey and me now! Haven't you? Haven't you? Dang, you are such a complete loser!

Dimeatone13: Now, wait a minute! I never said I was going to rat you guys out, and I never was! But, if you keep this attitude up, then I just might!

Bubbajoe699: So what, are you coming now?

Dimeatone13: Heck no! I don't want to get caught and end up in Juvenile Hall!

Bubbajoe699: That is why you don't get caught.

Dimeatone13: No! Ever since you have met that Casey dude, it has been burn this, steal that, toilet paper this house, key that car! Don't you understand? Don't you see what he is doing to you?

Bubbajoe699: What? What has he done?

Dimeatone13: He has made a huge impact in your life and altered it into cruelness.

Bubbajoe699: You are just jealous the he and I are becoming better friends.

Dimeatone13: I could care less right now about jealousy! I am not taking part in this immature foolishness! And if you know what's good for you, you won't go either. Or else you can forget about being friends.

Bubbajoe699: Alright, the only special person I can think of losing is my girlfriend! Goodbye! - Signed off (1:56 PM)

Dimeatone13: Bye to you then! - Signed off (1:56 PM)

Jamie J. Goldman – High school -- Lee High School, North East ISD

Tears were streaming from my mother's eyes, subtracing the tracks of her gummy mascara on her swollen eyelids, as she screeched down the neverending hallway, in terror. She dashed to abscond the wrath of the vicious predator in the maroon cloak. My own mother forgot about me. She left me isolated in her blinding dust as she sprints to safety. I was now the victim in the game of physical abuse. The massive figure, approaching promptly to my flaccid and weak body, grasped the earlobe of my right ear, dragged me for thirty-seven seconds, and then repunched and beat me severely on my own bed. With the only possible arm strength left to use, I grabbed the G34 revolver, the one resting on my cherry wood bureau and shot him in the heart.

"Bzzz, do you love me!?" danced and rang the silliest 1999 edition alarm clock as it vibrated back and forth on my pillow, and sang its bubbly tune. I never put the alarm clock on my desk, or I would never wake up. The alarm clock was my only hope to awake me upon every dreadful school day, so it slept with me, on my pillow. The scent of burnt waffles engulged the only oxygen left in my lovely abode. Same routine every morning. Take my last gulp of orange juice, and retrieve to the bus stop, "the transportation for the retardation." You know, that comment always was a bit too derogatory for my wit, intellect, and attitude. What I didn't know, was that at 3:49 of January 31, 2005, my whole world would change before my eyes.

I grinned with dismay when my mother pleaded to me to be the ring-bearer at George's and her wedding.

"Sure," agreeing ever so kindly to be a part of this disaster.

I was completely inept to the situation at hand, and I grew very curious with my usual dosage of the vague questions that begin with "Why?"

"Why did you leave Dad, why did you two fight, why am I crying for no reason, why are you appearing so vindictive Mom, Dad, why are you staying out too late?" My parents could only reply with "I'm sorry James, but it's all over, no more." I blamed myself for the divorce for years until I gave up at the custody battle and saw my future being with my mother. "Goodbye, Dad." I stole away from his tense hand grab.

George was my stepfather, a man always to his word, honest, and a very thriving and prosperous psychologist. The other night, the moonlight shining to create humiliating spotlights upon the people who creep within the late hours, George came home in a fiery rage. George was fired and labeled as a "psycho." My stunning mother, willing to sacrifice everything for the two men she loves, including me, fixed George's usual drink, to relax.

The cognac on the rocks, on this special night, had trouble mixing with the chemicals that lurk in my stepfather's mind and brain. The chemicals would contrast and drive him insane, this suspenseful evening, and they did. The imbalance only endured for four complete hours.

George slapped my mother across the face, and her cheek split open to reveal many torn vessels. She was hit vigorously and it began to storm heavy, stinging droplets of precipitation. I took action as the only true man in this house. I had to protect George though his maroon doctor cloak would intimidate me, but it only pushed me further to rid my family of the scoundrel. My mother abandoned our manor and ran straight for the closest police station. George, shaking each of my fragile limbs, believed with such faith that my mom and him were finally threw with me. I striked back with a bullet to his chest.

I sat in the pouring rain, an accomplished and worthy man, with the choice of self-defense in the situation, and I began to bawl. I thought to myself, "I l-l-o-ove you Mom, and m-miss y-o-ou Dad." Everything is gonna be all right.

69

Arianne slouched into class, eyes cast down and sorrow emanating from her in colossal waves with each sluggish step. Kat quickly saw the grey clouds floating about her head threatening to burst and spew dark and heavy rain. She sat down in her chair beside Kat, her face taking on a last look of defiance before she crumpled and cried.

Kat, her protective instincts going wild at the sight of her friend's pain, turned to her to ask with a suppressed, nearly overwhelming concern "What's wrong?"

She waited with a forced patience as Arianne gathered herself. "Steven won't talk to me anymore. He won't even look at me or be in the same room as me." Her voice shook as she spoke and another tear raced down her cheek before falling to her desk.

Kat understood immediately and though she tried to fight it off, a great rage swelled inside of her. Steven had found out about Arianne's feelings about him, then pretended to love her in return. Then, he proceeded to ignore her for a week before waltzing back into her life as if nothing had ever happened to wound their relationship.

"You need to confront him," Kat said fiercely, trying and failing to maintain a calm and steady tone. She always got worked up when her friends were in need and she couldn't save them. "Tell him it's over. Get him out of your life for good. You deserve better."

"But," Arianne replied in a faltering voice, "I can't," In a whisper she added, "I love him."

"You can!" Kat's eyes were now ablaze. "You can and you have to. I'd do it for you but it's not my place. You can do it. I know it."

A lethal glance from their English teacher ended what their conversation and they turned forward to avoid conflict. Kat snuck a glance at her friend from the corner of her eye. Arianne's fist brushed away the tears and her face adopted a hard and determined look to it.

The next day before class Kat sat in her seat, her foot bouncing impatiently, waiting for Arianne's arrival. There she was! Arianne entered the room with her usual grace, a great improvement from the previous day's zombie-like motion. She wasn't glowing but yesterday's storm clouds had been blown away. Kat smiled with relief; she looked so much better. She was rewarded by a smile in return from Arianne.

"Talked to Steven," she said with a sort of grim satisfaction. She then, much to Kat's surprise, wrapped her friend up in a warm embrace.

"What was that for?"

"I wouldn't have told if not for you. Thanks."

"But I didn't-,"Kat broke off mid sentence.

Arianne flashed a brilliant smile.

"Kitty, you're the only one who told me I could do it. Everyone sympathized but no one tried in the least to help. If not for you I'd still by crying, waiting for him to talk to me again."

"If you listened, you girls might have better grades," Mr. Watkins growled.

Arianne and Kat snapped to attention. As she had the day before, Kat snuck a peak at Arianne. She was looking at the board, not seeing the words at all, smiling with radiance.

70

Michael Hill - High school -- O'Connor High School, Northside ISD

The sun was surrounded by a diverse spectrum of colors as it ducked behind the distant horizon; a deep red hue filled the bottom of the orange skies while purple stripes stretched under the clouds. It was a beautiful evening for a race. I was sitting on a bench in front of the racetrack, gazing at the dazzling sunset. As I sat, I began to prepare myself mentally for the race I would soon compete in. I was a runner. I loved to run. And this race would strengthen my energy and confidence. After the sun had lowered completely out of sight, my attention shifted to the racetrack. It was a round racing track of dirt, winding around a great circular median. Though the track itself was fairly short, it seemed to be very large and intimidating, having a sea of soil for its ground and illuminated only by the fading lamp of the sun. In only a few short minutes, I would step upon the track and attempt to overcome every one of my opponents. But as I stared at the path of dirt, I began to worry. Was I capable of running this race? Initially, I believed that I was, because I was a runner. I loved to run. But after seeing some of my opponents, who sported powerful muscles and enormous legs, I began to ask myself. Am I a racer? There was no doubt in my mind that I could run. But racing, a fierce competition, was a different matter. Just then as I was questioning my abilities, I saw one of the other racers enter the track. His shoulders were very broad, and his muscles were visible from a distance. He wore an expression of intensity as he jogged along the track, dripping with sweat. As I observed his movements, I realized that his image was very different from mine. I was no athlete. I was no racer. My body was so very small, and my mind was naïve and humble. How could I win a race against the fierce conqueror I saw on the racetrack? It seemed impossible. Redirecting my attention to the brilliant sunset, I felt a wave of hopelessness fall over me. Winning this race would be a fantasy, for I was so small and everyone else was so ferocious.

"Ready for this race?" I heard an unfamiliar voice say. Looking to my left, I saw who had spoken. It was a man I had never seen before, clad in a white suit and white hat. As soon as he had asked me this question, I was at a loss for words. While saying that I was ready would be a lie, speaking my feelings to a stranger seemed very odd. However, I ultimately decided to respond honestly.

"No, not at all," I answered, looking at the racetrack while some of the other competitors walked onto it. "Look at them--They're all so big, so powerful, and very determined. Look at me--I'm so small and timid." I looked at the stranger intently--he did the same to me.

"Are you suggesting that you're afraid of losing?" he inquired after a long gap of silence. "Does that mean you're concerned about the outcome of the race?" in addition to his white attire, the man was covered in white whiskers, and his eyes reflected great wisdom while he spoke. I pondered to myself. Was I afraid of losing? Is that what drained my confidence?

"If so," continued the man. "Then you are mistaken about something. The only way you can fail in this race is to run it as if you have no chance. You must compete with a sense of courage, valor, and perseverance." He glanced into the colorful sky. "Race like you're going to win," he added quietly, with finality, shortly after these words, I was summoned to the racetrack. And as I walked to the starting line, I thought of his words, I was summoned to the racetrack. Could it really be that easy? Was that all I need to triumph? Hesitantly, I crouched at the starting line, next to a man wielding a checkered flag. All at once, the man swiped the flag swiftly through the air. It was time to run. I burst off the starting line and instantly realized that each of my opponents was already far ahead of me. That could have marked the end of the race for me. But with nothing to lose, I decided to take the advice of the white-suited man: Race like you're going to win. I started sprinting across the track, immediately feeling a surge of energy pump through me. It felt odd at first, putting my best efforts into a contest I could not win. But after a minute or two, I began to feel truly exhilarated with happiness. As I dashed on, I was surrounded by an aura of thrilling excitement. I understood now; if I raced as if I were to dominate the competition, nothing could defeat me, not even loss. And though I did end up finishing in last place, I was mentally pacified, I had given the race my all. What more could be asked for? The same sense of joy followed me as I exited the racetrack, surveying the magnificently colorful sky. Never would I forget the race, for I had won.

71

Adam Ionescu – High school -- O'Connor High School, Northside ISD

Both our aspirations and our memories are products of the comprehensive, tangible reality that we exist in. From this, one can conclude that aspirations and memories must, hypothetically, share certain similarities. It is, however evident it may be, the secret goal of all who question the world that we live in to discover purpose in our individual existence. The location in which the discovery of this truth takes place will forever remain at least a memory to them. For some, it is a near-death experience; for others, such as myself, it is simply realization of the importance of relationships as a result of the recognition of sublime nature.

As a young boy, I was always fond of the heavens and frequently went out to an old prairie house my grandparents used to own to look at the stars through my telescope. My most valuable "possession" is something everyone sees and feels every day. Many hold different opinions of the night sky, but I can never produce a logical reason they have that opinion. Even as a young boy, viewing the various distant constellations and planets fascinated me. It was a religion. It imbued me with a sense and feeling of knowledge, although I hadn't really learned anything at all. I felt as if I was more real and connected to the world than I had previously been. It is this feeling, this sensation, that makes the stars a special place for me.

The word "home" is one all too often misused. A home is more than just a place that you eat, sleep, and do your homework in. It is evident that the culture of the United States differences greatly in comparison to the rest of the world. One thing that is the most abstract about our way of life is the view of the home and family. In a rural, fishing town in Costa Rica exists the true knowledge of these words. When I visited this small, tight-knit community the most humble people I had ever met, I was filled with the same ecstasy I felt when viewing the stars. It was a truly diverse way of life. My host family mother, or as they say, "mama tica, and her two kids, Priscilla and Gabriel, 12 and 7, woke up every morning at 5 A.M. just to say goodbye to me as I left for my Spanish classes at the local school. This simple act of kindness was but a stream in the Niagara Falls of warm-heartedness that existed there.

It is experiences and places in which we feel love in its most rudimentary form that people are connected to and hold deepest in their hearts.

She leaned against an old brick wall and stared blankly out into the street, slowly taking drags from her cigarette. She thought to herself amongst the honking and cursing of taxi cab drivers. This wasn't her idea of the life she'd always dreamed of, but she was making it. Right? She looked helplessly at her cigarette and took another drag, in hopes of finding comfort in the poisonous nicotine she inhaled. Some where she had gone wrong, she was just too afraid to admit it. Why was a lonely sixteen year old spending a lovely afternoon like this? She shifted her weight, looked up into the clear blue sky and put out her cigarette. With her hands in her pockets, she started down the sidewalk to the place she called home.

She arrived to a stained pine wood door. She opened it slowly, closed it with ease, and hurried up the stairs to her room, avoiding any kind of communication with her parents. She got to her room, her sanctuary, and fell on the bed. She looked at her pastel pink phone and touched the cord with her fingers. She ran her hand along the smooth plastic neck and picked it up. She put it back down. Who would she call anyway? She needed to hear a voice; anyone's but the one inside her head. She picked the phone up once again and dialed a familiar number.

"Hello?"

"Hey … Kat?"

"Hey Mel, what's up?"

"Oh nothing, um, I was just wondering if you'd want to come hang out with me and a few of my friends tonight, I'll pick you up."

"Yea, that sounds great!"

"Alright cool. I'll pick you up at seven."

And just like that, the voice was replaced with a dial tone. With a sigh, Mel decided to read until it was time to pick up Kat.

Around seven, Mel pulled up to a rustic stone house and honked. Kat dashed out wearing (as usual) her biggest, brightest smile. She hopped in the passenger's seat, and the two were off!

Kat had no idea where they were going, but she hadn't been worried until Mel pulled up into a dark alleyway in the city. Kat nervously got out of the car, not quite sure of what to expect. Mel locked the car, causing it to honk in reply. The sound echoed off the cold, wet walls that surrounded the girls. Kat followed Mel, about fifty feet down the alley where they encountered two boys and another girl. Almost immediately, Mel and the strangers lit up. Kat stepped back; this didn't smell like cigarette smoke to her. She gazed in wild wonder as she watched her friend swallow pills down with alcohol and shoot up suspicious drugs. What was going on? She saw Mel's face turn pale and her eyes roll back. She had to help her. In an instant, Kat began flinging her arms and grabbed at Mel.

"We've got to get out of here!" She kept screaming. She managed to drag Mel alone to the car, and lay her in the back seat. Kat rushed to the drivers seat and pushed on the gas, she was going to the hospital . . .

. . . Mel woke up to bright lights. She looked around in a daze, and found her hand clasped in Kat's. Kat had fallen asleep like that in the chair. Mel's eyes began to swell with tears that eventually formed rivers on her cheeks. What had she done? No one had ever been there for her like Kat had; no one had ever cared. Although she was asleep, Mel whispered to Kat, "I'm so sorry. I'll never do anything to hurt you like this again. You'll never know how much you mean to me. You've changed my life. You've saved me . . ."

73

Jessica N. Lopez – High school -- Lee High School, North East ISD

She sat there awhile, deciding what she would do next. The heat of the day stuck to her like her pink cami shirt stuck to her back, sweat fussing the two. Maybe if I stare long enough the answer will come to me, she thought. She had been sitting outside the door for a long time. The concrete curb that passed as her seat was warming up. Quickly she got up, passed over to the door and went inside. Never once did she look back at her friend who still sat on the curb.

High noon sun passed and the brushstrokes of dusk were setting in when she finally emerged from the house. Her friend ran to her. Her own eyes kept low to the ground, afraid to look up. They walked down the road and continued till they reached the corner store in silence. Then there against the side of the building, one girl demanded answers. "What happened to you in there?" one girl stated. No response came, only gentle tears from her eyes flowed. And as if by some mutual understand they both knew, but neither was about to say. "Kira, what does it mean when someone you think really loves you…" She couldn't go on, heaves of sobs and wails consumed the rest of the day. Kira never knew the rest of the question or what she was supposed to do with a friend who was raped. After that day, Kira and May never spoke of it again. May confessed to her parents three days later and Kira never saw her again. They were supposed to be best friends, and now May was moving to another town. "It would be all for the best if you no longer speak with May, even letters," May's mother told Kira shortly after they moved on the phone. "This has been a very disturbing event and May needs time for herself," she continued. "But what May needed right now was a friend, a real friend, someone who knows what happened. Kira couldn't just do that, leave her friend. With what money she had left from Christmas, Kira got a taxi and went to May. But when she arrived at May's new house, no one was there. The house lay empty as if no one had even bought it in the first place. Kira climbed back into the taxi and headed home, grief stricken that her best friend was out there in the world alone.

Some time later Kira finally did receive a letter from May. She was living in Ohio and apparently having a great time. She said that after the court hearing and Thomas was put away, she finally was able to get on with her life. Her letter ended shortly by just stating she was fine and she would write back again soon. Kira could not believe what she was reading. Words like "fine" and "great" were not words Kira expected to read for a girl who was raped three months ago. This letter has to be a lie, Kira thought aloud, there's no way she could really be feeling like this. And she wasn't. In reality, May was torn up, inside and out. She had become the talk of the town, even the town she moved to. Her mom wasn't the most subtle person, May was going to frequent visits with a therapist and spent her time alone on the weekends. She often thought about Kira and how things were going but according to her mom, Kira didn't want to be friends with her any more. May was no longer a happy child any more but a paranoid teen, growing to be a even more paranoid adult. May and her parents moved two more times that year before moving back to their hometown. This was perhaps the biggest step for her. She didn't return to school till her senior year and remained home school till then. Kira had heard the rumor of May back in town and sought her out. It was a reunion to remember, filled with tears, hugs, and ice cream. May and Kira talked that entire night and well into the morning. May told Kira of all the things she had seen and been told by her therapist. "It wasn't my fault, even though I thought so for a long time," May explained. "What do you mean," Kira asked. "Well my therapist says that I made the most important choice by saying <u>no</u> , and Thomas wouldn't take that, so he forced me. I had no will," May said. Kira sat there in awe, for the girl she had grown up with her whole life was now growing up without her. But it was okay, Kira decided because at least now she had her best friend back and they could grow up together again. "You know what though," May said. "What? Kira responded. "I think the most important choice I shouldn't have made was to go inside," she said. There was a moment of silence again like the day it all happened. And as if by some mutual understanding they both knew, but neither was about to say.

(Disclaimer: all names were changed to protect the identity of those in this story.)

I was fifteen when I fell in love for the first time. Of course, fifteen was a first for a lot of things. I was fifteen when I smoked my first cigarette; and I was fifteen when I first lost all respect for myself. Of course none of this was my fault. I just wanted him to love me.

Being a sophomore at a school of 5,000 students, I may as well have been seen any of the numerous birds that flew overhead at lunch time. I was sad, repressed and felt completely alone. And there I met a boy. No a boy. The boy. It's quite humorous, looking back that love blinds you to the world's realities. He was two years older, and in high school, that only means one thing. And everybody warned me about it.

When you love someone, you want them next to you as much as possible. I was willing to do anything to keep Mark by my side. He, of course didn't mind. He wasn't shy about telling me what to listen to, who to talk to, what to war, and even what to eat. So I became his dream. A skinny vegetarian, music obsessed and completely infatuated girl.

My longing for him to say "I love you" turned my world upside down. Allison, my best friend since fifth grade school, told me she didn't know me anymore. I didn't dwell on it. I was too busy getting high with Mark to really care about anything. I lost myself in his image. I forgot what even made me love him in the first place. I ignored what he was doing in my life.

The summer of 2001 was a huge blur of drugs, sex and Mark. He would be going to college in the fall and I was desperately clinging on. So many high school girls getting dumped when boys go to college, and I refused to be one of them. We sat in his care one afternoon, the windows rolled down, smoking our day's last cigarettes. It was a hot July day when he looked at me and said everything I had heard before in movies, books, and TV, and in the girls locker room.

"Megan, I want to see other people." He went on and on, about college, and changes, and maturity, but I wasn't listening. I was looking at the past 10 months of my life and mentally kicking myself.

"Mark, shut up and take me home." And he did just that. And slowly I began to realize Megan was gone. I got home, went to my room and tried to piece my life back together. I was left with a tortured soul, but also with the knowledge that people should not control me and my life choices the way Mark did.

Shelby McBee – High school -- Lee High School, North East ISD

At the beginning of the second semester of my 8th grade year, I was presented with a potentially remarkable opportunity, which led up to a difficult yet important decision on my part. In my English classes, I was known for my writing prowess. The teachers that had me even in years past bragged constantly about how good I was. There was even a time when my name and the mere term "writer" were synonymous. I had never heard of the North East School of the Arts (NESA) program, but it intrigued me from the get-go. It was said to have a special major for those who found creative writing to be their passion. It was certainly mine. Things looked great. I was eager to apply, along with other friends of mine.

There was only one problem: the magnet school NESA was located at Lee High School. Hailing from the Roosevelt High School area, I was upset that I wouldn't be going where I had originally intended to go. My father, after learning of my original intentions, was very reluctant to give NESA the slightest chance. He went to Roosevelt himself, along with his brother and sister. He felt a rather strong sense of school and family pride, and literally considered it "traitorous" that I merely considered straying from my original path. Roosevelt had its perks. There were two magnet schools there, one which I had thought about applying for. The Design and Technology Academy (DATA) seemed like a fitting place for me as well. I was highly gifted in math, and had an affinity for computers. Plus, scores of "nerdy people" were bound to be there, a group which I fit in with nearly perfectly. My family had gone there, and in a way I wished to keep the spirit living on. Most of all, nearly every single one of the friends I regularly associated with were Roosevelt bound for their own reasons. To go to NESA would mean to have a sort of "social rebooting." I feared losing the many friendships I had gained over the years, as well as how I would fit in at a school where hardly anyone knew me. I was a strange and eccentric child, and strange and eccentric children usually like being with those of their own kind.

My mother chose to encourage me, no matter what path I decided to take. She simply did not pressure me as much as my father did. So in the end, I chose to apply partially to rebel against my father and make a name for myself elsewhere, partially because I felt my knack for writing would not ever reach maturity unless I nurtured it as the program offered. When I found out that I was accepted, I was overjoyed. My entire family was pleased, including my father. I could now say I was on my way to achieving greatness in writing, albeit at the cost of having to practically start all over with my social life.

However, such things were proven to not necessarily be true. I did become a NESA creative writer (and still am to this day), but with a sacrifice significantly smaller than what I had expected. I was not the only one from my middle school heading for NESA, and not even the only one destined to become a creative writer. Alongside those, I have made scores of new friends and quite an interesting name for myself (admittedly, I am the "chick in the cape.") I still keep in touch with my Roosevelt friends and have acquired new ones over there as well. My family couldn't be prouder of me. Going to NESA was a very important decision that I made, and it has paid off more than well.

76

Annalicia McCumba – High school -- Lee High School, North East ISD

I have known Bryan for years, ever since I was a toddler. Although I don't remember much from our childhood, we have become good friends since then.

When we were kids, we didn't hang out much. I can only remember one time when we went to Six Flags Fiesta Texas, I was about 6 years old, and my favorite Goosebumps hat flew off of my head on the Road Runner roller coaster. I thought I had lost my favorite hat forever, but luckily Bryan was sitting a few rows behind me and caught it when his hands were up in the air. I was so happy that day. Since then, right up until December of 2005, we hadn't really spoken much. He went on his way and I went on mine. On December 10, 2005 my mother had gotten invited to a birthday party. This caused a conflict because that night I had made plans with my friends to go out to the movies. I ended up having to go to the party first, then after my mom would drop me off at the movie theater. When we got there I realized it was his mother's, Josie's, birthday party and I automatically started to look around for him. Once we spotted each other, we talked for what seemed like hours catching up on old times and telling each other what we had been up to for the past 10 years. He told me he had joined the U.S. ARMY and would be leaving in mid-January to Basic Infantry Training in Ft. Benning, GA. In between that time, right up until the point before he left, we became really close. It was then when we started to develop a relationship with each other. Before this time, I was the kind of person who appeared to be strong on the outside but was really weak on the inside. I couldn't function by myself and had to depend on other people to help get me through. I could be away from a person for so long before "losing" it, and here I was entering into a relationship with a person who would be so many miles away in a different state. As time slowly crept along, I developed a deep caring for him that I had not experienced before, which scared me a little because it was something I wasn't used to. Everything was going good right up until about late June. All good things come to an end sometime right? Our long distance relationship only lasted for about 4 months, but during that time Bryan taught me something that changed my life entirely. Throughout the course of our time together, there were moments when I felt as if I couldn't handle being in the relationship and doubting the feelings I had for him. I talked to Bryan about these feelings I was having and he always responded in the same way, "Stay strong, Anna, for the both of us. I need you to stay strong for me…please." Eventually I overcame my weakness, but sadly that's when it ended. Our relationship came to a sudden halt and it was time for the both of us to move.

In a weird way, he taught me to believe in myself, and made me a stronger person both inside and out. It made my life change for the better, and my outlook on life, friendship, and love became more positive. I don't dwell anymore on all the bad things that have happened to me. I don't live in the past anymore trying to relive moments that are long gone. I now believe in myself and believe I am a strong young woman who has a lot of courage and can achieve anything I put my mind to. I don't need to depend on anyone anymore. I'm done with that. I've changed for the better and, Bryan, I thank you for that.

Travis Moncus – Grade 10 -- O'Connor High School, Northside ISD

Christmas Eve, 9:00, Granddad's bed time, farmers go to bed early to wake up early. Granddad always says early to bed, early to rise. Christmas Eve at my Granddad's house is always the same. Everyone is in bed by 9:15 to wake up to the smell of bacon and eggs with biscuits and gravy, my grandma's specialty. So my aunts and uncles went to their rooms leaving all the kids on the cold couches in the living room. Me, I'm not a heavy sleeper and can't fall asleep with the heater crackling in my ear, right next to my couch. My couch is old, pink, with green flowers like design on it. I'm one of the smaller ones, leaving me with the smallest couch doesn't leave my cousins feeling bad. The year was 1995, and I was 7 years old. In my eyes I was old enough to know better, but still too young to care. I was a pretty quick kid. People make an impact in your life every day, you have to be smart enough to notice them.

I got up from my couch and sat Indian style on the cold tile floor to warm my little body. I was a tanned boy with golden brown hair. My Grandma called me her "Golden Boy". In the back of my mind I remembered that my grandma had made chocolate pudding. I got up and walked across the cold tile floor that almost felt like it was burning my small feet. I quickly opened the refrigerator and tried not to wake anybody I reached in and grabbed the pudding. I closed the refrigerator and reached with my weak arms into the clean dishes in the left part of the sink. A chill went through me when I picked up the freezing spoon. I walked over to the big oval shaped table and sat at the end where my Granddad perpetually sits at every meal. I have always wanted to be just like him, pretty big shoes to fill; since I can remember he has always been my hero, the man that could never die.

I took a few bites out of my chocolate heaven when I heard a low pitched click, I knew who and what it was. Unusually my Granddad was up and he had locked the bathroom door. You see the bathroom is connected to his bedroom and the table is right outside both of them, and with the thin, rotten, wooden walls in the pristine house, you can hear anything that makes the smallest noises. Even my little feet slapping across the tile floor could be heard, had someone been listening.

From inside the bathroom I heard a rattling noise like pills in a little bottle. I could almost vision him in front of the sink, a cup of warm water, taking a pill for his heart problems. All at once I stopped eating the pudding and sucked on my spoon. I began to think about the next morning when I heard a fist hit the wall from inside the bathroom. I got scared hoping, wishing someone would wake up to help. No one did. I could hear him gasping for air inside the bathroom. I twisted the handle it was locked. I stabbed the long end of the spoon into the crack of the door where I could see light, and it unlocked. With my weak innocent arms I through the door opened and looked inside. It was my most feared imaginable thing possible. My hero not breathing on the bathroom floor with one hand in the dry tub and the other holding the empty tube of pills palm up I did the only thing I knew to do. I quickly got next to him on the floor and yelled at the top of my lungs. "Help !!!" All at once lights came on in the house. Everyone filled up the bathroom to see me hugging my granddaddy's chest with tears running down my red face and soaking his white tshirt. I had never been so scared in my life, I was just a boy.

My dad and two of my uncles, in nothing but their Christmas pajamas carried my granddad to the truck and took off to the hospital. Me and my grandmother followed them. When we got there it was close to 2 o'clock in the morning, Christmas Day. My mother really didn't want me to go, but I didn't give her much of a choice. I slept in the chair next to my granddad's hospital bed. When I woke up Christmas morning to a beeping noise I had a gray, itchy hospital blanket, and a white sheeted pillow to lay my head down on. I looked over not really aware of where I was and saw my granddad on a long skinny bed with a white hospital gown on. My eyes began to swell up until I saw the monitor with his heartbeat showing. I stood on the chair, kissed his forehead and whispered "Merry Christmas." I saw a tear roll down his dry red face. The doctor came in and I wiped the tear away. He told me if we had gotten there any later he wouldn't be breathing right now. He also said I was a bright boy.

My granddad told me that no one had ever done something for him that meant as much as what I had done. My hero died this past Christmas left me knowing that no one else would make as big an impact on me or my life as he did. I just hope he will be waiting for me when my day comes so we can spend it in paradise.

78

The Arrogant, Dumfounded Dog Who Looks Like A Lizard.

One upon a time in down town San Antonio, there was a dog named Smokey. He would roam the streets day and night, all through out the city. He was an average size poodle. His hair was a very curly grayish blue, and he had on a hot pink and lime green bandanna around his neck. There was nothing anybody could say to him that would make him timid. The only obstacle in his way was that he looked like a lizard. This is a very extraordinary trait for such a popular dog. People would laugh at him continually when they saw him. This made Smokey very somber. One day walking through the northside of town, Smokey came across a little girl named Hayley. She was the cutest thing Smokey had ever seen. Hayley was nine years old. She had blonde curly hair with the bluest eyes. When Hayley saw Smokey she felt sorrowful for him. Hayley and Smokey became best friends. They would go to the mall, the park, and even Petco to go try on all the new bandannas they had. One afternoon while they were at the park Hayley told Smokey that she couldn't spend time with him anymore because she was moving to Dallas. Smokey was crushed. After Hayley moved to Dallas, Smokey would walk through the park unaccompanied by anyone and would soon become very ill. He desired to see Hayley one last time. Hayley came back to San Antonio to visit Smokey, but soon found out that he was very ill. Hayley spent everyday with Smokey in the hospital. Eventually Smokey got better, because now that Hayley was there he had something to fight for. Hayley and Smokey played once again in the park they had played in before Hayley left. Hayley told Smokey that she couldn't stay, but that she would visit him monthly. Smokey was so gleeful that he leaped for joy. So from that point on Hayley would visit Smokey every month and they would play in the same park every time.

The Winds of November

It was a bitterly cold day of an even colder month. It was on a Tuesday in November, the day she was diagnosed. My brother and I drove home from school both yet unaware of the events to come. From what I remember it was the wind that made it cold, but my recollections of that day still has trouble playing back in my mind. I gazed out the car window on the ride home; and even with the stereo blaring I could think just fine. I stared at fallen leaves soaring in the November wind, wondering if one day I could be like them. If I could be free, not held down by anything or anyone. My father was sitting on the front porch with a look on his face I had not seen in a long time. When my brother and I stepped up to the front porch he told us the news. "Your mother went to the doctor today and … the cancer has returned … except this time it's terminal." My brother almost fell to the ground out of remorse and shock. My mother was in bed upstairs and the walk to her room was the longest of my life. Every blistering step brought me closer to painful reality that in less than two months my mother would be gone. I stepped slowly into the room with a blank stare on my face, and through all her pain she smiled at me. At this I felt relieved, for this showed me that she was not afraid. We never addressed the illness directly and never mentioned the creeping future.

For two months I lied by her side, playing guitar and singing songs I had written for her, never had I seen my mom happier than those last months. Towards the end her energy began to fade along with her smile and the light in her eyes. The pain was too much to bear for her; her time was approaching. I lie at her side the morning of Tuesday December 24 and what she said next I shall never forget. She said, "Don't worry. I'm not afraid to die. I find it peaceful and lovely sort of. I will finally be free of all the pain, like a leaf blowing in the open wind. The only pain I'll be left with is the pain of never seeing you or your brother again. I want you to always enjoy life and live every day to the fullest because you will never know when life will through you a curve ball and a routine doctor's visit tells you that you have two months to live. You need to always be free and never let anyone hold you down or hold you back. I love you both." At this, my mother let out her last breaths and a small tear fell from her eye.

She was buried on Dec 26, my parents anniversary. Both my brother and I took her final words to heart. My brother is in his third year at United States Military Academy at West Point, and is soon to be married. I never have let anyone or anything hold me down from my dreams. I am the free leaf blowing in the winds of November soaring above it all.

Dear Mom,

Remember that time you saved me? You saved me from taking my life. I was on the floor of my room with a gun crying. I remember it well you came home early that day and heard me sobbing like a baby. I remember you opening my door and not moving. It looked like you were an ice cube. You didn't say anything for a second you simply stood there and took in what was happening. The first word you said was "Wait." You said "wait a second." You didn't tell me not to do it you simply wanted to talk to me first and let me know how you felt about me.

I remember you say "let's talk" just hoping that I would listen and I would hear the words that came from your heart. You told me all the things that I had to live for and how some girl isn't worth "checking out early." I'll never forget that saying; those three simple words. I've never heard someone talk about suicide like that. I remember us talking for about two or three hours just sitting there on my bedroom floor, that wooden floor was so stiff and cold that day. I don't know how we sat there so long without noticing how uncomfortable it was until afterwards.

I guess all in all, Mom, I just needed to say thank you for everything. For keeping me safe and saving me from Satan and from myself most of all. God gives us hope and that day you proved that to me thanks.

Your loving son,

Daniel

An article I read once in history spoke of places that are special to an individual. The locations that force your hair to stand on end. The room that gives you goose bumps. The article referred to places where wars occurred throughout history, but its meaning was clear and present. People often feel connected to places where different events took place throughout their lives. The presence of those around you at the time of the memory is strong and real. One is hurled through time into the past and forced to remember when they visit one of these "special places."

For me, it's my grandmother's kitchen. I can feel the room's warmth generating from the stove turned on high heat. The heater didn't suffice in the colder of the winter months. The colorful drawings and pictures on the refrigerator are illuminated by the orange glow of the Virgin of Guadalupe candles. The room was filled with the scent of the cat food, and a faint purring could be detected as the white and brown feline tiptoed by, back arched softly rubbing its silky fur along your leg. There was a missing tile on the cold floor where my grandpa dropped his hammer while trying to repair the cabinets the summer before. My initials on every chair leg and doorknob made my possessive six-year-old personality obvious. I can still smell the menudo cooking in the "big silver pot." We used that pot for three occasions. Menudo and tamales were cooked for Christmas, Easter, and Thanksgiving.

It was the kitchen I grew up in. Making cascarones was always a favorite of mine. I loved making the glue from flour and water and stuffing confetti into the delicate eggs. Mother's Day gifts were always crafted at my grandma's kitchen table. Father's Day ties were wrapped on the wooden eating area.

My grandma's kitchen is my special place. It's where most of memories were born. It's where my height was recorded, where the cat scratched my hand that was forever scarred, and where I was when I heard the news of the birth of my two younger siblings.

A person often feels connected to a place because their memories reside there. Without memories, one has no childhood, and without childhood, one has no joy. Life's greatness is too often measured by the number of breaths a person takes rather than the number of moments that takes a person's breath away. Memories tie us to such moments. Special places allow us to revisit and relive them. Without such moments and memories our lives become mundane and empty. As a wise man, (Ferris Bueller), once said, "Life moves pretty fast. If you don't stop and take a look around once in a while, you could miss it."

As I floated aimlessly down the river, laying ever so gently on my mother's chest, everything so quiet in the late afternoon heat, I couldn't help but to be happy. My skin, hot from the brutal Texas sun, was cooled by the water droplets evaporating off my back. You might find it hard to believe that a young kid filled with so much energy can have a good time just laying around. But I had been bouncing around all day, and all I really wanted now was to do nothing. My eventful day of jumping off rocks, and swinging off of rope swings into the chilled haven of the river, had left my body worn out and my mind drained. The water flowing past the tube that we were laying on made an eerily hypnotizing and relaxing sound, and it was making my very drowsy. As I fell into a sort of half sleep, I found myself praying. Unconsciously, I prayed for this river that was supplying my entertainment for the week. I prayed that it would run strong for me the rest of my life as it had done for my dad and his parents before him. So far it hasn't failed me yet. And now instead of going once a year to this scenic getaway, we can go whenever we want. My grandparents realized my dreams, and their dreams as well, of the future of this river, and they decided they wanted to be a part of it. So they bought some land and a house there on the banks of that great landmark. To me that house is the greatest place in the world, and I wouldn't give it up for anything. I can only hope that one day I will be able to sit in the cool water and talk to my kids and grandkids the way that my parents and grandparents got to do. So whenever I visit my favorite place in the world, I always find myself praying. And when I'm not there, I find myself wanting to return.

Beep!

wolfgirl94: Hey! Hvnt talked in a while.

Beep!

DJzombie64: Wow! Hw r u?

Beep!

wolfgirl94: Nt 2 good. Zack just broke up wit me @ the Spot.

Beep!

DJzombie64: …I'm sry…

Beep! Beep! Beep!

wolfgirl94: Nt ur fault.

wolfgirl94: Nd that's nt evn wat hurts the most!

wolfgirl94: It's the fact that he did it there! Of all places! Y there?

Beep!

DJzombie64: That is rather cruel.

Beep!

wolfgirl94: I dn't even want 2 go back there anymore. That's hw bad it is!

Beep! Beep!

DJzombie64: Hold up.

DJzombie64: U can't do that.

Beep!

DJzombie64: Zack was a jerk 4 doing this, but u can't gve up just like that.
                        Then, he wins.

Beep!

wolfgirl94: …

Beep!

DJzombie64: Didnt u hve ur 1st kiss there?

Beep!

wolfgirl94: Yeah. Wit Josh Alexander.

Beep!

DJzombie64: Nd do u remember wen we were lil nd we used 2 pretend 2 make
                        a witch's brew nd dance on the shore?

Beep!

wolfgirl94: Yeah. LOL. We were crazy kids.

Beep!

DJzombie64: Do u remember wen I "Married" Paul Jacobs?

Beep!

wolfgirl94: Yes! LOL! U stool ur mom's wedding dress nd ruined it wen u
                        fell in the mud! Paul ended up "divorcing" u the next day!

Beep!

DJzombie64: U see. It's more than just a place 2 us. We practically grew-up
                        there. I often wish I had more time 2 visit it there.

Beep! Beep!

wolfgirl94: Let's!

wolfgirl94: The nxt time u come out. We can go there nd shw Gabe it.

Beep!

DJzombie64: …ok. We can talk more about it then 2. Gabe is alwys asking about
                        my childhood.

84

Essays
with
Craft Lessons

85

Noah Alonzo -- Little Hero
Type of Mini-lesson: Dialogue limitation

Writers combine dialogue with action.

Noah gracefully combines speech between two people with action all around both.

Activity:
Look at the 4th paragraph. Here's Noah's pattern:

> Speech – speaker 1
> Speech – speaker 2
> Action
> Speech – speaker 1
> Action

Challenge:
Try inserting a pattern just like that into your own writing.

86

A Time to Help

I have experienced a lot of things in my life. One by one, I see amazing things happen. I remember the most amazing thing that ever happened to me…I saved someone. It began late one night, when everyone was asleep. My mom drove around a corner, then my mom and I stared at a building on fire. "Uh oh," I thought.

My mom pulled over and got out of the car and told me to get out too. "Mom, what do you think happened?" I asked. "I don't know," she replied. "Heeeeelp!" someone inside the building yelled. "Mom, sorry I'm doing this, but I've got to save that person!" I stated. "Son, no!" she screamed, but I was already in the building.

The flames felt as hot as the sun, actually the flames felt hotter than the sun! "How am I going to find someone in here?" I asked myself. "Help! Help!" someone yelled. "Lucky me," I whispered. I sprinted to a closet guarded by flames. Luckily, I found a pail of water and put out the fire. Then I opened the door and spied a scared girl sitting in a corner of the closet.

"Sorry, but we have to go," I stated. "OK," she whispered. We ran faster than the speed of light. As we ran, I could hear the building coming down behind us. "Faster!" I yelled. Then we jumped out a window on the middle floor. For a moment, my heart stopped. Just when all hope was lost, two firemen saved us.

Beep, beep, beep went my heart on the scale. "Where am I?" I asked. "You're in the hospital," my mom answered. "Is she OK?" I asked. "Yes, she is, now get some rest, you need it you little hero," she replied.

Kendra Copenhaver -- Hobby Lobby Bunny
Type of Mini-lesson: Modifiers that describe

Writers use all kinds of different ways to describe.

Kendra uses an amazing variety of modifiers: adjectives, multiple adjectives, hyphenated adjectives, crisp verbs, and similes.

Activity:
        Activity Option 1: <u>Group Race</u>
            Find 3 similes
            2 multiple adjectives
            2 single adjectives
            2 crisp verbs
            2 hyphenated adjectives
        Activity Option 2: <u>Dull it up!</u>
            Group rewrite one paragraph, without any adjectives or describing words. Read them out loud.

Challenge:
Try using a variety of describers in your piece.

88

The Time I Helped a Desperate Friend

I galloped into a pleasant classroom, spotted a weeping woman and wondered, "What happened?" A dear friend of mine had a tragedy happen to her. Two vicious robbers snuck into her delightful house and stole everything but her family's clothes. If this happened to me, I would be bawling my eyes out, but this friend was as happy as a lark.

When I had first heard this terrible news, I ran as fast as a cheetah to hug her. I knew she was devastated but she didn't want to show it. When I got back to my uncomfortable seat, I prayed to the Lord that he would comfort her and her family. A dirty, wet tear fell from my eye, and pinched my cheek, as I thought about what happened to my joyful friend. She and her mom trotted out of the colorful room, thinking about what happened.

When I finally got home, I whizzed into my extremely messy room. "What happened in here?" "It looks like a hurricane flew by." "Clean it up right this instant!" roared my angry mom. "Maybe later, I have to write a card to someone first," I replied. I was very befuddled because I didn't know what to write or draw. Finally, it hit me, I could just write what would make her feel better. I drew teenie-weenie hearts and grandiose hearts.

All I need to do now is buy her something. So I thought, "What would make her feel safe at night?" A stuffed animal would. Me, my polite mother, my groovy sister, and my goofy aunt trekked to Hobby Lobby. We saw millions of precious stuffed animals, but only one caught my eye. It was a medium-sized bunny that was as cute as a baby. The next day, she received the gift. I will never forget how happy she was!

Now I know that a small thing can make a huge difference. I know that the bunny had touched her heart. Everybody in my class said they would do something. No one did. I was the only one. That's what a true friend does.

Elizabeth Cummins -- The Cliffs

Type of Mini-lesson: Snapshot

Writers use "snapshots" to convey complete visual images to their readers.

Elizabeth expertly describes her surrounding, with a perfect example of a well-wrought snapshot just at a highly dramatic moment.

Activity:

Highlight the visual images in this paper. Compare notes.

Challenge:

Try writing a "snapshot" of what you see at some point in your own writing.

For more on Barry Lane's Snapshots, see *The Revisor's Toolbox* and visit www.discoverwriting.com

---

90

In the Cliffs

"EAT MY DUST, SUCKER!" I yelled over my shoulder so Robin could hear me. We darted past Bill's house as if we were gazelles in a stampede. Too bad Bill is dead now, because he was a really nice guy.

But Robin just happened to interrupt my thoughts by yelling "NEVER!" Robin and I had started a race. There were strategies racing through my mind of how to get further than she will. Then it hit me! I should run and climb all the way up the cliffs. I had started to climb the cliffs by the time Robin caught up to me. Our little race had become an adventure.

"OW!" I whined. I pricked my finger on a thorn as sharp as a knife. I sucked on it until I got it to stop hurting, then I told Robin "My blood tastes salty." We both couldn't keep from laughing. We started climbing again, but this time with caution. Somehow we managed to get too high for comfort. Robin has always been afraid of heights. I wasn't usually afraid, but this time I was. I looked down to find any footholds, but my eyes snapped shut. I made myself open them again and surveyed the cliff side. I saw some roots shaped like little hoops coming out of the cliff side. I tested my weight on each root. I managed to find a comfortable position holding onto 3 of the roots. My feet were on 2 of them, and I held on to the last one with my right hand. I stood up and helped Robin onto some of the other roots directing her with my left hand. We climbed the rest of the way down the same way we got up. We were back to safety. I looked up to where I was and trembled at the sight. Quickly I checked if Robin was okay. Then I checked if I was okay. It all added up to scraped hands and sore feet. I of course can't forget a spanking from my mom.

That's how I learned my lesson to stay out of trouble and put other people first. "Thank you, thank you, thank you very much."

--Quote Elvis Presley

91

Jodi Davis -- Neighbor's Fire
Type of Mini-lesson: Kernel summary (compare)

Writers move from one main thought or action to another, in paragraphs.

Jodi's writing is so tightly organized that it's clear to see the author's planning.

Activity:
In groups or as a class, write a one-sentence summary of each paragraph. You'll end up with five sentences, or a kernel essay. Read the five sentences aloud to see if it's a short version of the essay.

Challenge:
Try this with your own piece. It can help you tighten up your organization.

Fire, Fire!

Splat! The ice cream man whacked a scoop of jellybean ice cream on my gooey waffle cone. I gave the man two dollars, and strolled out the door. As I got on the block, my jaw dropped as well as my ice cream. Smoke was everywhere! I suddenly noticed my neighbor's house was smoking!

I ran as fast as lightning into my house. I eyed my family and screamed, "The neighbor's house is smoking!" Me and family ran outside. The terrifying smoke jumped to the clouds. My dad banged on the door in panic. The neighbors burst through the door. But, their daughter was trapped! I banged on her door. She stepped back as I lifted up her window. I clutched her in my arms and trolleyed her to her family. Everyone was safe. But, the house wasn't. As quick as a wink, the smoke turned to fire! I rushed quickly into my house and called 911!

Honk, Honk! The red as a rose fire engine sped around the corner. I was so excited! I had never seen a fire truck in action! Eight brave firemen jumped out of the car and rescued the neighbor's cat Lucy, and their dog Lola. One climbed to the top of the ladder, and started spraying the house. The fire was out in a jiffy. As the unharmed men came toward us, we clapped and cheered. The heroes introduced themselves to us. But, after minutes of talking the firemen congratulated me! They said, if I didn't see the smoke, the house would of turned to ashes. Then, came a great reward!

The firemen put me on a roller coaster ride to the top of the ladder. I could see the whole town! A photographer for our local newspaper took a picture of me and the firemen. It was posted on the front page the next day! Then my neighbors took me to get some jellybean ice cream!

The day was very tiring, but way out of this world! Many people wanted to hear my story. I spent hours telling everyone. Now I know that, doing things for people, is better than receiving things from others because saving my neighbors made me feel good inside. Try helping someone around you, I guarantee, you'll have a ball!

Kimberly Drinkwater -- Waikiki Lifeguard
Type of Mini-lesson: Plot complication

Writers don't just tell what happened, and what else happened. They make a story more interesting by throwing in roadblocks, or complications.

Kimberly smoothly develops her plot by telling what could have (but didn't) happen, to complicated her conflict. This adds so much depth!

Activity: 1. Think about an accident or a mistake someone made in your story. (Something went wrong, so write what that was.)
2. Write one thing that would've solved it and why that didn't work.
3. Write another thing that would've solved it and why that didn't work.
4. Write what did solve it.

5. Look at Kimberly's piece, how Kimberly works two unsuccessful solutions into the first sentence of the second paragraph.

Challenge:
Consider adding "failure attempts" to any piece you create so that any problem you present is not easily solved.

94

Kimberly Drinkwater – Grade 4 -- Nolanville Elementary – Killeen ISD

A True Hero

Splash! Splash! Splash! My family and I were at Hawaii for summer vacation! We were at Waikiki Beach swimming and tanning in the beautiful sunlight! Everything and everyone was peaceful until…"Ahhh! Help! Help! I'm drowning!" a little girl screamed!

The little girl's parents were too far away to hear her scream, the lifeguard was also too busy because he was talking with his girlfriend, so I made a sacrifice! I ran into the sparkling, clear, blue water and swam to the little girl. Then I reached for her hand and swam to shore with Suzie, the little girl, on my back.

I didn't know what to do, so I let Suzie down and told my dad to get the lifeguard and Suzie's parents! When the lifeguard came and her parents came they were really worried! I saw the sad glare in her parents' eyes, and I couldn't stand it but to cry! The lifeguard did everything to help Suzie, but nothing happened!

I was so sad and scared that a little girl's life was about to be taken away, so I quickly ran to Suzie and tried talking to her. "Suzie, are you OK?" I said in a worried and shaky voice and suddenly her eyes slowly opened and she quietly whispered, "Yes!" I was so happy and excited tears were zooming down my cheeks!

Suzie hugged me and thanked me for saving her life! I was so proud and happy I helped someone! Then after all the drama, people told me, "You're a true hero!" I kept repeating the words they said in my mind and used the final hour to play with Suzie!

I knew that day I was a true hero and helped someone! I knew I did the right thing and if I didn't that girl wouldn't have a life anymore! I did not want an award either because my award was given from heart. I had pride and responsibility! I will never forget this day, when I learned the true meaning of being a hero and saving or helping a girl!

Thank you for giving me this great experience of how it's like to be a True Hero!

Alyson Holsey -- Milo

Type of Mini-lesson: Inner processes

> *Professional writers know that readers are not in problems that have easy solutions. Readers like to read about a character's confusion and attempts that fail, before reading about the solution.*
>
> *Alyson expertly shows confusion and many steps to figuring something out.*

Activity:

Highlight any phrases that show confusion or mental work of figuring out how to handle the situation.

Look at how the mental process happens, not at just the beginning or ending, but all the way through the piece.

Challenge:

Try adding your inner process, or the steps of figuring things out to your next piece.

96

As I stepped out of bed, I glanced at the note dangling from the door. I read it out loud, "Aly, once you finish your chores you can go outside, and please don't wake anyone here up. Not unless you bashed your head open."

I got dressed and did all of my chores. Once I stepped outside the door I saw a cinnamon colored footpath. It was never there before. The dirt path left me puzzled because each time I walked closer it looked like a train track. When I got there I came across a cat. She was so beautiful. The cat was as black as coal, and she had snowy white fur running down her body. It was as if she spilled milk all over herself. I came to understand that we were by a railroad track. It was golden, and it was so shiny that it burned my eyes just to look at it. It was cool the way the sun was blazing on the track to make it hurt people's eyes when they'd look at it. Being near the cat around this place filled me with gleaming joy from my head down to my toes. I did not want to tell anyone about this place, but then again I want to tell my friends. Otherwise I would have this whole magical place all to my own! I had decided to name the cat Milo. I like that name because Milo and Otis in the movies had adventures. I ran home to get meat and cheese and bologna to put in the blender. After that I ran to the place where Milo was. I gave her the cup that held her food. We heard a train coming and that scared Milo so she ran to the tracks which was really stupid and sure enough her two front paws got ran over. This only made her freak out worse. I ran quickly back home to get my needle and my thread. When I got to Milo nothing changed. She was still running around like a bird with one wing. I held Milo down and I sewed her up. I couldn't take them out until her skin grew together. I have to tell someone about Milo running on her back legs! I can't tell anyone because then they will know about this place. I hope her food is still there because she looks hungry! We ran back to see a wolf was eating Milo's food. I ran to the train track and tried with all my might to pull up the train track, but the stupid rim wouldn't budge so I got a fat piece of wood. I swung that thing like it was a snake. BINGO! Right upside the head. That only made him more mad! I swung it again. This time made him dizzy, so I swung it one more time popping his neck. The last time broke his back and that was that. It was pretty dark so I picked Milo up and I snuck her home.

This was a day that I helped Milo. I don't feel a bit disappointed. I used to be scared of wild animals but not now. Milo helped me too, you see. I guess that old saying is true help someone (or thing!) and they'll help you.

Anjelica Saj King -- Baby Bird Funeral

Type of Mini-lesson: Asides

Writers use asides to give more information (but usually just to whisper private secrets to the reader).

Saj uses several chatty and effective asides, punctuating them with parentheses, and adding voice and depth to this piece.

Activity:

1. Highlight the words and phrases in parentheses. These are called "asides."
2. Read the sentences around (without) the highlights.
3. Next read the sentences again, with the asides.
4. Talk about what you notice.

Challenge: Try adding several asides in your next piece of writing. You can write them while you're drafting the piece or add them as a revision step.

98

Have you ever helped someone? Don't lie to me, I know you have! Everyone has at some point in their life. Even you! And I have too. No kidding! More than once actually. Many times.

One of those many times was the one when I helped a bird. I found him/her in my back yard. A waterfall of tears cascaded from my eyes as it became clearer and clearer to me that this poor little fellow was dead. Every minute the bones seemed to creep further out of the little bird's lifeless body. The ants would jerk the skin and the flesh would slide off of bone like a curtain sliding off of the beginning of some gruesome, bloody play. Soon, the sight was so unbearable that I could not stand it any longer. I rushed inside, nearly ripping the door off its hinges in the hurry, and got a box. It was small, square, and the perfect size for my little friend. I carefully cut a piece of green foam about the size of my box, and set it there. I then put the lid of the box on top. Standing tiptoe on a chair (it was one of the chairs that spins, and was making me very nervous as I swirled about atop it) I finally managed to grab (well, more knock down) a huge box of cloth from the top of my mom's dresser. From it, I selected a piece of purple satin, and a piece of purple silk. These I carefully glued on top of my box. Then I grabbed it, and ran back outside, forgetting the mess in my rush. Then, I took one look at the bird, thought about having to touch it, and ran back inside to get my mom. When we were all back outside again, my mom gently picked up the bird and put him/her (I'm still not really sure…) into his/her casket. We then got out our shovels and dug a deep, deep hole. We carefully carried our little friend over to the hole, and bent down to place him in it. A single tear fell onto the little box before it was buried forever. A shell was set where he was buried, to remember him by. It is still there today. I feel like I did the right thing, putting him to rest. There's a real truism in that. A truism is a catchy little saying that tells the moral or life lesson of the story. Something like don't judge a book by its cover. Everything has a truism, and this story's truism is that you can always help someone even if they're not human!

99

Haley Chase Kinman -- Stinky Boys' Fire
Type of Mini-lesson: Kernel summary (compare)
(See Jodi Davis's essay and activities.)

Writers move from one main thought or action to another, in paragraphs.
Hailey's writing is also so tightly organized that it's clear to see the author's planning.

Activity:
In groups or as a class, write a one-sentence summary of each paragraph. You'll end up with five sentences, or a kernel essay. Read the five sentences aloud to see if it's a short version of the essay.

Challenge:
Compare Haley's kernel essay to Jodi Davis's. Then compare how the two authors developed their kernels in different ways.

100

My Terrifying Rescue

As I jigged down my street I spotted smoke rising in the air. Then I smelt a horrible scent. I thought "Oh my, there must be a fire!" Wait I better stop here the rest is kinda scary. Okay if you insist, I'll continue.

Just as I got to the house, I heard a earthshattering scream! Then it quickly faded. I realized what I had to do. So I took in what could have been my last breath and walked into the burning house. I yelled out "If you can hear me yell as loud as you can!" There was no reply, only silence. Then an idea came to me, the little kid probably fainted from the heat. I was right, it was terrifying, but at last I found the little girl passed out on the bathroom floor. I was relieved to get out of the house.

After fifteen minutes the girl woke up. I explained that her house had been on fire and that she fainted. She started to remember things right then. She told me that her house smelled like stinky boys so she tried to light a three-wick candle. Well you probably know the rest of the story. Then out of nowhere a TV guy showed up to interview me! I was delighted to explain the story. I was excited to be a hero!!

Finally we found out that the mother had went on a quick errand and left her child alone. I cannot tell you how many times the little girl thanked me. I got a reward from the mother of $100,000. She was being very generous. By the time the mother returned the house had crumbled down, but she was grateful anyway.

This story teaches a great lesson. If you see that someone is in trouble help them. Do the right thing and go help someone today! Now I know that helping makes a huge difference!!

101

Justin Marsh -- Mimi's Garden

Type of Mini-lesson: Surprising words (modifiers)

Writers often surprise their readers by putting words together unexpectedly.

Justin uses some strikingly surprising words, creating a fresh experience for the reader.

Activity:
Read this piece and highlight any words you did not expect to hear. Compare highlights with your classmates.

Challenge:
Think about inserting some "true but surprising" words into your writing.

Justin Marsh – Grade 4 -- Nolanville Elementary – Killeen ISD

I once thought that I could not be a helpful person until….

As the morning sun glared into my shallow colored eyes, I told myself repeatedly, I do not have chores today. Then I remembered how much everyone admires my brother for how helpful he is and how my family calls him helpful boy and not me because they think I am lazy. When I'd try I break something or mess up, and if I mess up, my brother does it and no one will give me another chance. I whispered to myself, he is not any different than I am. Then a sound of a door slamming shut interrupted my jealous thoughts about my brother. I spun around and faced where the sound came from, there standing in a pleasing position, was my mimi in her gardening suit with two shovels, flowers inside a nonheavy pot, and a long water hose. She asked sweetly if I could help dig a hole for the flowers and help rinse and plant them. Suddenly I felt as if I had butterflies in my stomach. I was more nervous when I told myself here's my chance to be helpful, so I answered my mimi I will help you. She sweetly commanded me to follow her so I marched behind her.

I followed her into her garden, she stopped in the middle of her garden, and got down on her hands and knees, I sat and listened, as she softly spoke, Stab your shovel into the dirt, and lift the shovel back up and put the dirt to the side. I picked up the shovel and did what she told me to do. She whispered start digging. I started to dig, then I started thrashing with the shovel as glob of dirt flew up. Finally soil was in the hole. That's when I stopped and ran to the water hose, I picked it up and ran to the flowers and squeezed the squirt button inside the flower. I picked up the flower and put it in the hole, and scraped the dirt back over the pot and filled up the hole. When I picked myself up I noticed that mimi was watching me smiling and told me I did good. Now I know I can be very helpful to not only my mimi, but everyone.

103

Anna Matthias -- The Bunny Escape

Type of Mini-lesson: Sensory Words

Writers don't use every strategy they know, all the time. They pick and choose whatever works best for each situation.

Anna treats her readers to a masterful flurry of noise, not from beginning to end, but just when the story truly gets noisy.

Activity:
Read the piece.
Highlight the words and phrases that bring sounds to a reader's imaginary ear.
Notice where those words and phrases are concentrated.
Examples: thrash, squeaking, squaking, screeching, crowing whistling, whispered.

Challenge:
Find (or build) a moment in your own writing where there's a sensory flurry. Add enough sensory words so that a reader's imaginary senses feel it.

The Bunny Escape

A few weeks ago I went to my favorite place, Pet Works. I was just there to visit then the bunny got loose! I had to help the lady at the counter catch her, and the bunny's name is Lulu by the way. Here's the story.

It was just after school and my dad was dropping me off at Pet Works.

"Bye dad, see you at five o'clock!" I yelled.

I sprinted up the sidewalk and flung open the door. "Oh, my gosh." the place was a reck! "Hello?" Nobody was in site. Suddenly, Jamie, the counter lady, appered behind a huge stack of dog beds, carrying a net. "What's that big net for Jamie?" I curiously asked. "Lulu is loose somewhere in the store. Will you help me find her?" Jamie replied. "Of course I'll help, but I don't need a net." I said looking at Jamie with curious eyes.

So we started shearching around the store. I was looking behind some dog food when there Lulu sat. Before I could grab her or even call out Jamie's name she was off. She ran like lighting bouncing off the walls like a rubber or a bouncy ball. Jamie ran in the room after having no luck in the bird and fish room. She got one glance of Lulu and immediatly started to try and catch her in the net. She tried for 30 minutes but had no luck. Now it was my turn.

I grabbed the net from Jamie and started swinging like mad. Then….tharash!! I hit the net as hard as I could on the ground. It made Lulu stop running. It made the mice stop squeaking. It even made the birds stop squaking, screeching, crowing, and whistling. "Nows your chance Anna. Catch her." Jamie whispered in my ear. So I raised the net and lowered it in two seconds. I didn't catch her.

Lulu was ten or fifteen feet away now. So I ran and flung the net, and ran, I ran and flung a gillian times more. I was so tired out I could not walk! Then suddenly… Plop! She landed right in my arms.

"Jamie, Jamie, Jamie! I caught her! I caught Lulu!" "How?" she asked. "I just stood there and she hopped in my arms!" I replied back. "Wow." was all Jamie could say.

After we put Lulu in her cage and made sure it was locked, we heard Beep! Beep! "Oh, that's my dad Jamie. Gotta go! By!" I said and ran out the door.

I climbed in the car and as we drove off "I will always remember when I helped Jamie catch Lulu the bunny at Pet Works," I thought secretly to myself. And I never forgot.

105

Kennedy Read -- Etnie

Type of Mini-lesson: Creating reader curiosity

Writers don't answer every question the reader has, not at first. In fact, writers often try to create questions in the reader's head, and answer them later.

Kennedy plants some information which creates one big question. The story unfolds smoothly but is more interesting because of the mental puzzle the author creates.

Activity:
Highlight the words and phrases that reveal any information about Etnie.

Challenge:
Take a look at something you have written.
Think about planting clues by taking out some explanations, and choosing where to reveal your answers.

106

Helping Hands

"Ummm," I moaned as my sister Chloe was yelling "Wake up, wake up." I finally forced myself to slither like a snake out of my bed, and stomp into the living room. I saw my family sleepily searching it and thought "What's all the commotion about?" After a few minutes I shouted "What's going on?" My dad answered, "Chloe lost Etnie again." "Not again," I cried as I rubbed my head. Yes again, Chloe replied sassily, and this time he is long gone. Don't worry "I will help you," I chimed in.

Once I grabbed on some clothes, I asked Chloe to retrace her steps. "Ummm" let me see, well first I…um oh I first went to the park. Off to the park we go I said. We ran as fast as lightning there was no time to spare. We looked all around, the swing, monkey bars, slide, and seesaw. No sign of Chloe's fluffy friend.

Next I…I went to Holly's house to play. Well, "why don't we look there" I exclaimed. Holly was sitting on her wooden swing when we arrived. "Hey," she shouted as she jumped out of the swing. "We lost Etnie again," I sighed. We were wondering if you have seen him." "No but you are welcome to look around." "Thanks," I said in a tone that sounded happier than a mouse with a piece of cheese. We checked everywhere we could think of but still no sign of Etnie.

It was getting late and still no news of Etnie, Chloe's favorite animal. I told Chloe it was time to go home. After a few hours of looking at the house it was time for bed. Chloe climbed in her comforting bed. But wait she felt something at the bottom of her bed, she pulled it out it was Etnie. "Yea," she yelled. Now I know to never give up until you have searched everywhere.

107

Cherilyn Song -- Wizard of Oz
Type of Mini-lesson: Sequel to a movie

Writers often borrow from well-known stories and write new versions of old stories or some new variation.

Cherilyn crafts a sequel episode for The Wizard of Oz, borrowing Dorothy and the Wicked Witch. This is how she proves her central thought or truism.

Activity:
1. Read the piece.
2. Identify how much of the story came from *The Wizard of Oz*. Of these, highlight the most important words and phrases yellow.
3. Identify the parts that Cherilyn invented. Of these, highlight the most important words and phrases blue.
4. Identify the truism that this story proves. Highlight it green.

Challenge:
 Choose a truism of your own.

Try writing a sequel to a well known story or movie to prove your truism.

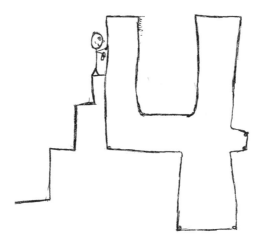

108

Do you know the story of <u>The Wizard of Oz</u>, when Dorothy meets strange creatures, and they help her get things for the Witch and then return home? Well, that was just part one. The story that I'm about to tell you is the other half that tells you the whole thing.

It was a rainy Saturday morning, when I was cheerfully eating my Cinnamon Toast Crunch, reading <u>The Wizard of Oz</u> book. Suddenly, like a snap of a finger, my glistening silver spoon anxiously came to life. It grumpily cried out, "Hurry up and make a wish in five, four, three," I had to think quick. The words "Go inside the book with Dorothy!" just rolled out of my tongue. All of a sudden a blue light mist surrounded me, and it forced me up the breakfast table, and into the maroon colored book. It felt like I was being pulled into a magnet. With such effort, it seemed my body was about to shatter into a million pieces. My feet soon had a surprisingly great shock wave, as it safely landed on a green pasture that was looking over a village called Honey Wheat Villa.

The confusing scene was such a blur, I didn't even realize that Dorothy in a blue calico dress was crying a river of tears onto the rich soil. Her cheeks were flustered with redness, while her eyes were flooded with salty liquid. After she had calmed down, I questioned the girl what was the matter. She slowly replied, "I succeeded on making my way towards home, but because I was hungry, I went to my favorite bakery shop-- Billy's Baking Delight. But when I entered, the whole place was in ruins! And there was the evil Witch standing in the middle of the shop, wearing a wicked grin!" I thought to myself, I wonder if the Witch had already known that Dorothy would visit the bakery, or was just a lucky guess?" I dumbfoundedly stared at the sobbing girl, until suddenly, I came up with a brilliant plan to get rid of the devastating Witch.

In my mind, I came up with a tremendous solution that'll make Dorothy explode out into space with happiness. Since the Witch hates sweet foods, such as frosting, we could get ten cans of that substance and squirt it all over the Witch's body. She will soon melt, while Dorothy and I will put her liquid-self into a jar. Then we'll throw it in the deep, blue sea to be lost forever. I told that to my new friend, and she instantly stopped her nonsense, a sly grin slowly starting on her shining face. The next day at dawn, the two of us went to the grocery shop and met at Billy's Baking Delight. We did just like what I had wanted it to go. After exactly fifty-nine minutes and fifty-nine seconds, it was a calamity in the room. But the peculiar thing is, smack dab in the middle, lay a still, black puddle of a melted, now gone Witch.

The point of the adventure that I had was to show you that helping someone doesn't always have to be evil, but it can also earn you friends.

Megan Weimorts -- Mittens

Type of Mini-lesson: Blending sentence functions

To tell a story, writers use mixtures of speaking, thinking, viewing, and doing.

Megan skillfully blends these four kinds of writing in her piece, leaving readers perfectly clear about the whole memory.

Activity:
     This highlighting can be done by groups.
Green: everything the narrator thought
Yellow: everything the narrator saw
Blue: everything that anyone said
Pink: all the action (not counting thinking or talking)
Share and compare what you notice.

Challenge:
Highlight something you've written in the same way, just to take a look at your own patterns.

110

As I walked up to my grandma's house, I saw my grandma. I thought to myself, "I wonder why she wants me to spend the night."

When I got up to the porch I waved bye to my mom and hugged my grandma. She said come in and set your bag down. I went in and did what she said. She offered me a glass of milk. Then she told me to follow her because she had something to show me. I put my milk down and did what she said. She opened a snowy white door and in there was so much sewing things I almost fell over. I was so shocked I could hardly say a word. She asked me if I wanted to help make mittens and I said yes. My grandma said we needed about six or seven pairs. We got the materials out and started working. She did one for example and showed me what it would look like when it's done. She brought in some band-aids just in case I accidentally poke myself with the needles. I grabbed the materials I needed and got to work. The first one didn't turn out too well, but I kept trying. After a little while I went to get a snack. When my grandma and I got in the kitchen I told my grandma that I already had three done. She said that I was pretty good for a six year old. Also she said that three was enough for today. That night when my grandma was asleep I crept into the sewing room to finish the mittens. When I was done with all the pairs of mittens I decided to make my grandma something. The next morning I gave my grandma a heart that had a picture of me on it. Above it said "I love you." Under the picture it said "By: Megan." My grandma said she liked it and then hung it up. After that we ate breakfast and then my grandma took me home. In the car she said thanks for helping.

I figured out that when my grandma let me help her I did something special for her because she let me.

Taylor Agan -- Guitar
Type of Mini-lesson: Time Transition

Writers take us on journeys through time, weaving between past and present without confusing the reader.

Taylor manages time shifts, flawlessly moving from present to past, then back to present.

Activity:
Highlight the words and phrases that show a time shift. Notice he has a memory from the past framed by the present time.

Challenge:
Try putting a time-shifting frame around one of your memories.

112

We all want to be rockstars, right? We all want to be rich, famous and really popular. Right?! Well I sure do! By the time I'm 20, I want everyone to know who I am. But, it isn't as easy as it looks to become famous. It's hard work! You have to build your way to the top. I don't want to brag or anything, but I'm a pretty good guitar player. But, I haven't always been this good. When I got my first guitar, I couldn't play half the things I can play now! We all have to start somewhere…

It was my 6th birthday and I was spending it with my great-grandparents. "Woohoo!" I thought as I ripped one present open after another. I had a pile of wrapping paper to my left, and a pile of presents to my right. I guess you can say I was spoiled. I loved the sound wrapping paper made when I ripped it off a present! RRRIIIPPP!!! It reminded me of lightning crashing in a thunderstorm! As I grabbed my last present from my grandmother, I noticed its funny shape. It looked kind of like a long deformed rock and it felt like it too. But, I didn't care. I just wanted to hear the incredible rip from the tearing of the wrapping paper!

I ripped the wrapping paper off the present, but didn't hear the familiar ripping sound. Instead, I heard a jumble of musical notes! It was a guitar! I held up my guitar for my grandparents to see, and they smiled at me like it was the proudest moment of their lives. I positioned the guitar in my lap, and slowly strummed the guitar. As I heard the strings harmonize, I let out a joyous laugh. Why, you ask? Because, on that day, I truly felt like a rockstar!

Now, seven years later, I am an awesome guitar player. I've even written my own music! Everyday, since I acquired my first guitar, I've been practicing. Practice makes perfect. Even though I've gotten new and better guitars over the years, I still have my first guitar. I keep it so I'll never forget how much you can improve if you put your mind and strength into. It doesn't matter who you are, or what you do for a living. There's a rockstar inside of everybody.

Sarah Cavanaugh – Dear Dalia
Type of Mini-lesson: Deepening a truism

Writers use all kinds of rhetorical devices to drive home a point, and sometimes they use combinations of devices.

Sarah crafts a powerful expansion of her simple truth here, weaving a pair of metaphors into an extended appositive.

Activity:
1. Find in your writing a simple, important truth.
2. Paraphrase that sentence.
3. Think of one metaphor, something that it's like from science.
4. Think of one metaphor, something that it's like from toys.
5. Put the two metaphors between the two other sentences.
6. Read your paragraph and see if you like it.

Then read Sarah's last paragraph.

Challenge:
Try that pattern in your writing!

114

Dear Dalia,

Do you remember when we were kids and we were both really bossy? We used to fight over who was right and who was wrong. Even though we were kids we still acted like we knew everything. But we didn't know that we would be the answer to each other's problems.

When we first met you were six and I was turning seven. I was outside coloring on the sidewalk. You came up to me and said, "Chalk is for the sidewalk and markers are for paper." No offense, but right then and there I wanted to slap you. Have you ever heard of first impressions? Because yours wasn't the best. You probably felt the same way with me. Don't worry, I would be freaked out too if I saw a kid coloring the sidewalk with Crayola markers.

Do you remember how your dad would come home drunk and yell at your mom? I remember it like it was crystal clear. Every time they would fight, you, your sister and I would pray from under your bed. Thank you for showing me that I was never alone. Now I know that God is always with us.

Field day at school was coming up and your dad said you couldn't go. There was no reason for you not to be able to go except your dad. He had to make everything put you down. It was like he was allergic to happiness. He would always say things like, "You're so ugly, you're as ugly as your fat mom," or, "No guy would ever like you." What's really sad is he put me down too. The first time we met he said, "So you're Dalia's little fat friend." It was time for us to defend ourselves.

"Dad, why don't you be nice for a change? Why do you always put me down? Just because you're not happy doesn't mean you have to ruin our lives because of it," clamored Dalia. For once he said he was sorry. And I felt great knowing I changed your relationship toward your dad.

From you teaching me that I am not alone, from me teaching you about courage. We complete each other. Even when we were kids we always knew something that the other one didn't. You are the nucleus to my cell. You are the missing piece to my puzzle. You are my best friend.

Love always,
Sarah Cavanaugh

Stefan Compton -- Dirt Bike

Type of Mini-lesson: Point of view, Absolutes

Writers create questions and tension using rhetorical devices like repetition and grammatical structures like absolutes.

Stefan uses a deep series of absolutes (sound ringing, vibrations shaking) together with 2nd person point of view which plunge the reader into physical participation. But there's a little mystery. This author doesn't let us know the exact cause of the sensations until the last two words of the introduction. And at that revealing moment, the author takes back the point of view, converting to 1st person.

Activity:
1. Read the first paragraph twice.
2. Highlight the absolutes.
3. Compare it to: Have you ever ridden a dirt bike? I have.

Challenge:
Try a 2nd person sensory barrage like this.

Online resource: for more on absolutes and other "brushstrokes" like it, visit Harry Noden's website: www3_uakron.edu/noden/

116

Vroom! The sound of the powerful motor ringing in your ears, the vibrations shaking your body. The wind pounding in every inch of your aching body. Rays of sun blinding you, through leaves of towering trees. The weight of thick plastic covering most of your, sweat drenched, thick polyester uniform. Your muscles aching from the constant jerking of a hundred and fifty pound beast. The exhaustion from the endless hours and every minute seeming as it were an hour. Your eyes peeled open for the unexpected, your mind dreading to blink, the dryness of your eyes causing a dreadful burning sensation throughout your face. Your heart beating from the adrenaline of swerving through a tedious path of rocks and dirty sand, sticks, nearly being decapitated by low hanging branches of solid trees. Focusing on avoiding the slightest mistake, for it could be the result of a great deal of pain or perhaps death. The fear of the unknown that lies ahead. This for me is a typical yet still amazing weekend riding my dirt bike.

This wonderful, incredible, unforgettable experience is the result of five years of strong determination and many challenging defeats of hurdles thrown towards myself, as I learned to master the sport of dirt bike racing. Five years previous to now, the thought of riding a dirt bike never occurred to me. Even though I admired almost everybody who had ever touched a dirt bike, I hadn't dreamed of riding one. However my thoughts on the subject were endless.

My step dad had introduced me to dirt bikes. He was a skilled and experienced rider. Whenever my parents had seen the way dirt bikes inspired me, they worked to make my dream of riding come true. When they first told me this I was both nervous and excited. I felt like there was a zoo in my stomach, no words could compare to the joy in my heart.

When I first started to learn, I was clueless. I would fall left and right. Even though I was constantly sore I practiced, as much as possible. The famous words, "Practice makes perfect" were constantly lingering through my head. Gradually I got better and better. My mind was focused on speed and oblivious to the possible consequences of my actions.

After about two years of raising the bar to heights of skill level, I never thought possible, I came to a big bump in the road. I had damaged my bike beyond repair, and to top that my parents were having a divorce. Only races away from the great pride of being a youth pro, it was over. My mom and I had to move and start over from scratch, no car, no house, no money.

Over the time of a couple of months, my future in dirt bikes had turned from the dark of night, to the light of day. My mother made the ultimate commitment and bought both of us new bikes. Even though I had lost much skill my dream to make it to the top was reborn, bigger, faster, and better than ever thought possible. I shall continue my adventure to the top, nearly a youth pro.

117

Logan Emerson -- Nightmare Swimming
Type of Mini-lesson: Transitions

Writers use not only transition words, but whole phrases and sentences to wind a reader through a thought process.

Logan's sentence-to-sentence transitions in the conclusion are masterful. They are so smooth they look easy.

Activity:
First, write this sentence, filling in the blank with something true:

> *I _____ more and more.*

Add this:

> *It has turned into _____.*

Add:

> *And if I ever had the chance,_____.*

Share short paragraphs.

Challenge:
Add this pattern to your collection of writing strategies. Be on the lookout for sentence patterns similar to Logan's.

118

Logan Emerson – Grade 7 -- Glenn Middle School, San Angelo ISD

When you learn to swim, your mind is filled with happiness. Swimming can be a competitive sport or just something to do for fun. One of my passions is to swim. Throughout my life I've swam either in a river, lake, pool, and when I was younger, the bathtub.

In the summer, about five years ago my family and I were having a big bar-be-que party. My mom let me swim in the lake, right where she could see me. She put my tiny arms through the pink floaties I got for my birthday. My dad carried me to the water and then set me in, dipping his feet right next to me. I held on tight to legs while he talked to my aunt Peggy. The pressure of the water sped up as I was trying to tell my daddy. I yelled, "Daddy help, look at the water!" My eyes got bigger as water covered me. I was carried away by the water. My feet soon got caught in a string of moss. I tried to get above the water but there was nothing to hold on to grab. Tears poured out of my eyes. I knew right then and there I was going to die. The next thing I saw was my daddy's face and his muscular arms surround me. I no longer felt the moss tangled around my leg. All I could feel was my mom's arms, never wanting to let go. Everyone surrounded me crying their hearts out. "Why is everyone so sad?" I asked myself. Then I thought that maybe someone died. From that night, until I was eight years old, I never even thought about swimming. I was too scared to face the water. The only place I swam was in my humongous Jacuzzi bathtub. But my plans of swimming changed when Coach Gotcher decided to give swimming lessons. I begged my parents not to sign the permission slip, but they wouldn't listen to me. They checked the yes box and gave me five dollars for the fee.

As we walked in the gate of the city pool, my eyes widened. All of the horrible memories were flashing back. I could not get over this. Coach Gotcher dove into the pool, beckoning for us to follow. I refused to even dip my toes in. Everyone sighed, knowing that I wouldn't go in the water. I stayed plenty far away hoping they wouldn't call me. But as Coach Gotcher walked in, my nightmare began. I walked nervously toward the pool of water. "Oh no, she's really going to make me get in the water," I thought to myself. I stepped down the ladder, with my feet shaking. Coach Gotcher told me to swim to her. "I think she is crazy, thinking that I'm going to let go of the ladder," I pondered. She swam over and grabbed my legs rotating them up then down back up and then down. She let go and my hands released the ladder. My eyes were sealed shut, but by golly I was swimming. Soon I bumped into the other end and quickly opened my eyes. I was in the deep end! Everyone clapped for me. "Yea!" I yelled. I splashed in amazement.

I swim more and more each day. It has turned into a hobby. And if I ever had the chance, I would turn myself into a mermaid.

119

Uriel Garcia -- Ironing

Type of Mini-lesson: Layering thinking

Writers let us inside their heads, telling us their thoughts as events happen.

Uriel uses remarkable inner speech, adding layers of thinking to his actions.

Activity:

Find a simple action sentence in your writing.

Ask yourself these questions, weaving the answers into your writing

What was I wondering?

What did I think would happen?

What were the only things I knew right then?

For a second, what did I think?

Read Uriel's third paragraph to see where the questions come from..

Challenge:

Try using mental questions like these on your next piece.

120

Uriel Garcia– Grade 7 -- Herman Furlough Middle School, Terrell ISD

Dear Mom,

You have taught me to do a lot. For example: tie my shoes, how to use the bathroom, comb my hair, and a lot of other things. But one thing I will never forget, I want to thank you for. I think you can remember, I was 8 yrs. old and it was on a Sunday. It was tough but I got it. I still do it to this very day. It was a sunny Sunday, we were getting ready for church. Everybody was rushing. I was in my room looking for something clean to wear.

I had already taken a shower, all I needed was something to wear. You came in and told me to hurry up. So I decided to go under my bed and get some clothing from there. That was where all the dirty clothes were. But you didn't know. I grabbed some pants and a shirt and put them on. They smelled dirty and were all wrinkly. I was on my way out of the room, when all of a sudden I get pushed right back in. It was you of course.

I was wondering why! You told me to take all the clothes off. I did as you said. For some reason I knew we were going to be late. Everybody else was out of the house and gone. I thought we weren't going to church, but you did. You told me to go to your room, get the iron and the ironing board. I took it to my room and turned it on. I only knew three things about it. That it was very hot, and heavy. For a second there, I thought you were going to iron my clothes.

You told me to iron my clothes and all the rest of the clothes under the bed. At the time I was really confused. I've only seen you and Domingo use it. The other thing that I knew was that it gets your clothes very straight. I seen my brother use it a lot. You told me to stay here. I was at the house doing nothing but ironing. I got tired, but I just kept going and going. It was 2:30 in the afternoon when you got home. Everybody else was at my aunt's house.

You came in to my room smiling. I thought you were just being sarcastic. But you weren't. You told me I did okay. But that I could do better. I was ready to drop dead. So I just lay down on my bed. You were telling me that if I ever try to go to church with my pants not ironed, that you were going to spank me. So I never did. It always seems that if I'm not doing something else I will probably be ironing.

As you already know, I still do iron. I would probably say that no one in the family could iron more better than me. Not even you, and you taught me. I'm always telling you that I could do better at the cleaners than you. Not really though! But my ironing ways sure have changed a lot. Domingo tells me that I iron in the funniest way, but hey, it gets the job done.

Well anyways, I just wanted to thank you for teaching me how to do something I never thought I would end up doing. Last Saturday at Patty's party, I ironed Domingo's pants with starch, it came out so crazy. It even had me amazed. Well you sure have taught me a lot in my life. I just wanted to say thank you. Thank you for everything you do for us, as a mom and wife.

Love,
Uriel Garcia

Sarah Jara -- Spelling Bee

Type of Mini-lesson: Dialogue with inner reactions

Writers weave their unspoken reactions to spoken dialogue, giving readers a rare glimpse at what goes on <u>inside</u> a person as well as outside.

Sarah narrates her mental reactions to the words spoken around her, giving the readers a chance to glimpse her insights and feelings.

Activity:
Look at a piece of your own writing or invent on a blank page.
Write two lines of dialogue, like this:

> You:
> Your friend:
> Write your mental reaction or what you thought about what your friend said.

Challenge:
Listen to Sarah's dialogue without any mental reactions.
Try this on your own writing.

122

"Your word is caper," she said. "Caper?" I repeated back. The pronouncer nodded patiently but her eyebrows furrowed in evident annoyance at my inability to just spell the word. I swallowed and then licked my lips. I had seen this word before in a book about pirates. I knew how to spell it! Slowly, but deliberately, I began to spell the word: "C-A-P-E-R, caper," I said. I didn't look toward the judge's table because I couldn't bear to see one of them reach over and pick up that little brass bell which, if rung, would indicate that I was out. But I did not hear the little brass bell ring, so I listened instead for those three magic words, the ones that, if said, meant I still had a chance…then I heard "That is correct."

I sat patiently in my chair as I looked around the saw many people in the stands talking amongst themselves in hushed voices. I leaned slightly to my right and whispered into my friend's ear, "I'm nervous." "Why?" she asked, "I mean you are the best speller in the class." It was true that I always made 100's on my spelling tests, but this was different. You didn't get to study the words in advance.

"Okay, ladies and gentlemen, if you'd please take your seats, we're about ready to begin the spelling bee," said the pronouncer. My stomach lurched at those words, and I felt like I might hurl; it was with that feeling that the spelling bee began. The words in the first few rounds were fairly easy, though some people got out. My friend, Bridgette, and I were still in, that is, until the fourth round. Bridgette walked up to the microphone, but she spelled her word too fast and missed a letter. The judges rang a little brass bell and Bridgette was out. I managed to stay in for the next two rounds by correctly spelling 'caper' and 'disengage.' Now only this short, blonde haired boy and I were left. The boy stepped up to the microphone haughtily and with great confidence. He made me feel anxious just sitting there. The boy's word was 'relevant,' but he spelled it RE-L-E-V-E-N-T. The brass bell rang and the boy sat down. I knew even if I spelled 'relevant' right, I'd have to spell another word correctly to win. I stood up and walked to the microphone as the pronouncer gave me the word again. I spelled it correctly and the butterflies in my stomach felt more excited than nervous. The pronouncer gave me my next word: "Endeavor," she said. The word was somewhat familiar, but I couldn't think of where I'd seen it before. My time was limited, so I gave it my best shot. "E-N-D-E-A-V-O-R," I said. I held my breath and strained my ears, and all I heard was three words…

I did win my school spelling bee and I went on to county where I placed second. I've never gone further than that in any other spelling bee before or after that time, but spelling remains, to this day, to be something I'm really good at, something I've learned that I do well.

Zachary Lara – Outfield Grass
Type of Mini-lesson: Anadiplosis

Writers use rhetorical devices of all kinds for all kinds of effects on the reader.

Zachary uses a device called anadiplosis in the words of his first sentence.

Activity:
Read Zachary's first sentence. What do you notice about it?
(It's two sentences. The last word of the first sentence is the first word of the second sentence.)
Circle the repeated word. This is called an anadiplosis, or that thing that Zachary did.

Challenge:
Try one in your own writing. Find a truism in your opening or closing, and try turning it into a truism chain, like Zachary's.

Online resource: for more on rhetorical devices, visit an amazing website, www.americanrhetoric.com.

124

Zachary Lara – Grade 7 -- Glenn Middle School, San Angelo ISD

Dedication: it leads to hard work and hard work teaches you to do something well. And that's pretty much where my story begins. With dedication and hard work.

It all started ever since I was little. My dad would take me to a park to work on my skills, daily. Whether it was just learning to field a ground ball or learning to crow hop to easily throw out a runner from the outfield, he taught me how to. I remember going out to the fields and every time I smelt that elegant smell of the outfield grass, or felt the rocks and the dirt from the infield slide across my body as I dove for another ball thinking, "Good job. Way to give it your all!" I love that. For some reason I love the pain of the rocks. Some people hate it, but to me, it's like a high dollar massage. And for me, I'd rather be in a hundred degree weather working my rear off than in some water park, any day. That's because I have a dream. I dream that I will go to the University of Texas in Austin to play baseball for the Longhorns on a full scholarship. Then, I will go to the pros and become a Hall of Fame baseball legend. That's my dream and I'm willing to do anything to reach my dream. I practice as much as I can to be a better athlete.

A few years ago while I was in Little League it was spring break and we had one more game, plus if you had made the All Stars, you would have that. And as spring break came my parents were talking about where we wanted to go. And when they asked me I said, "Nowhere, I want to stay here and practice so I can make All Stars." So while everyone else was on vacation, I was at the fields practicing my heart out. I would stay there and learn how to do all kinds of things that I never even knew existed. I learned to drop step, back hand, forehand, and all kinds of stuff. And when spring break was over and we had our game, I amazed everyone there with my fielding. The next week or so I was in my room and my dad called me and said, "Zach, guess what? You made All Stars!" I was so happy. My dad also told me that they said my fielding was amazing! It felt so good to know that somebody else thought that you learned how to field better than anyone else.

So, you always need to remember this. Let nothing stand in the way of you and your dreams. Practice hard and give it your all. If you do just that not only will you achieve your dream, but you will also end up mastering that skill.

Colton Lathram – Radio Baseball

Type of Mini-lesson: Embedding other types of text, genre

Writers use all kinds of writing in their pieces.

Colton begins his piece with the words of a baseball announcer. The readers get the feeling of listening to the radio, hearing a game.

Activity:
Read aloud the first paragraph.
Mark the spot where the radio stops and Colton takes over in first person.

Challenge:
Try inserting a news account or reporter's version somewhere in your piece.

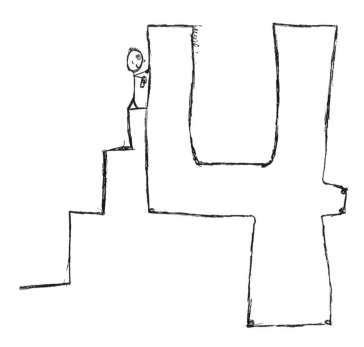

Colton Lathram- Grade 7 -- Alamo Junior School, Midland ISD

"Crack" Colton Lathram hammered that ball," the announcer howled, "As Colton rounds first and looks for second, the outfielders are still runnig towerds the ball. "I can't believe it," the announcer yelled is shock, "He heading for third." The ball is on it's way to the infield from the outfield. Colton slides into third and he's..."safe." The announcer explodes with excitement because winning run is now on third and Luke is up. Luke is batting 2 for 2 today and all we need is a base hit to win. Luke hits a screaming grounder in the hole and Colton scores. "The Mavericks win! The Maverick win!" The announcer screams. I, Colton Lathram, have learned many things about baseball over the years I've played. My parent told me that when I first learned how to walk I walked straight to a baseball and through it as far as I could. I didn't throw it very far but as young as I was, a few feet was pretty far.

I think watching my brother play baseball inspired me to play. My brother played for the Lee Rebels in High School. He played first base and batted about 7th or 8th in the lineup. He was alway number ten and so am I.

My dad coached most of my teams from Teeball all the way to American League. He tought me everything there is to know about baseball. He tought me how to pitch, how to hit, how to field grounder, and everything else. My dad tought me how to pitch in the windup and from the stretch. Beside playing in Little League I also played select. Select is where you can lead off from the bases. My dad tought me how to lead off and how to pick the runners off. The pitcher must be in the stretch in order to pick someone off. The runner leads off and the pitcher tries to make a pickoff move to throw someone out before they can get back to the base. If you balk the runner gets to go to the next base. A balk is when you make a move that is not allowed while a runner is on base.

Swinging a bat was one of the hardest things to learn. Even now I mess up on some of my swings. Most of the time I pull my left shoulder out, so I don't hit the ball solid. Instead they turned out to be little grounders. My dad also tells me I step out or dip. Step out means that when I step to swing I step to the left, instead of staight at the pitcher. Dip means that when I swing I swing low. When I dip I'm usually under the ball or I hit the bottom half of the ball and hit a fly ball. Lately at practice, I've been hitting line drives or solid ground balls.

Pitching is my favorite position on the field. but it is also one of the hardest and most pressuring. I have three pitches: a fastball, a palmball, and a curveball. My dad tought me how to throw all three of these pitches without hurting my arm. I can through a fast ball around 65 to 70 miles per hour. It is pretty hard to hit. He also told me that my legs are a big part in how fast I throw it. I have had a hard time throwing my palmball where I want it so I don't throw it to often. My favorite pitch is my curveball. If I throw it right the batter will swing and miss or hit a little grounder to the first baseman. If I throw my curveball the correct way it is almost sure to curve about half a foot. When the catcher calls the pitches one finger stands for fastball, two fingers stands for curveball, and three fingers stand for palmball. If I don't want to throw the pitch he gives me I shake my head no. Then he will change to a different pitch until I find the one I want. Then I shake my head yes.

If I may say so myself, I think I have the best pickoff moves on the Mavericks. Except to first base Luke has the best move because he is left-handed. Last year, I had the most pick off in a single game out of my team. My dad tought me all the pick moves there are. My best move is to second. I got the runner almost every time.

I am really good at baseball and I have learned all of it from my dad. I've learned to never settle for less than your best because I would never had made it this far in baseball if I hadn't given it my best.

Madison Watson -- Losing Gabby

Type of Mini-lesson: Abruptness for power

Writers startle readers with short or direct sentences, making an emotional impact even stronger.

Madison sets up lovely, smooth and graceful openings to each paragraph until the last one.

Activity:

Highlight the beginning phrases in each paragraph (from indention to comma or period). Read just these parts out loud. They are all smooth transitions, until the last one. The last one is direct and powerful. The contrast creates harshness, which impacts the reader.

Challenge:

Consider using introductory phrases and clauses on sentences <u>EXCEPT</u> the most painful ones.

128

Through all the devastating things that have happened in the world, have you learned anything? From Nine-Eleven, the Tsunami, Pearl Harbor, war, or death? How, how the world has changed!

Through the uncountable lessons life has taught me, one has stuck extremely well. When my little sister was diagnosed with cancer; she taught me to care.

"She has brain cancer." Dr. Gearheart told my family. Silence sweats the outside of me, but I was screaming inside, NO! "She has no longer than a month, you may see her if you would like." Joining hands, my family entered the hospital room. Just the look of her was too much, tubes going into numerous places on her pale body; sweet, young Gabby, was fading away.

Weaving my way through the flowers and "Get Well Soon" balloons, I took her hand. "I love you sissy," she whispered. "I love you too," I sobbed. How can my perfect, beautiful, ten-year-old sister be dying? She hasn't even really got to live? As my parents went through surgery options with the doctors, I continued to think and pray.

It was then that Gabby, as it seemed, read my mind and softly whispered, "Maddie, life can't last forever, love it and live." That one sentence is and always will be engraved in my head.

While I was pondering that, a Bible verse popped into my head. Isaiah 29:11 says, "For I know the plans I have for you, plans to give you a hope and a future." It was then, that I realized all of this was happening for a reason. I recited the verse to Gabby; she smiled and weakly murmured, "I like that!"

Without either of us knowing, Gabby was teaching me something that I will never forget. I never, ever thought that someone younger than me could teach me a life lesson so powerful.

Gabby's time ended on the day of love, February 14, 2005; I was devastated. Although through the time she was alive I grew stronger and better in caring for others. The longer I live, the more I will care.

Brad Ballinger – Big Brothers

Type of Mini-lesson: Genre switch: journal entries

Writers used to tell stories mostly written as straight narratives, with events in sequential order. Nowadays, writers often use other forms to spice up their storytelling.

Brad tells his story through a sequence of journal entries.

Activity:
Read this essay.
Out loud, summarize what Brad's ordinary narrative might have said if Brad had not used the journal format.

Challenge:
Look at a narrative you've written.
Could it be re-told in journal entries?
Try one this way.

130

Brad A Ballinger – High school -- O'Connor High School, Northside ISD

June 5, 20xx - Dear Journal,

Man that sounds so hokey. "Dear Journal." I hate this. Mom's making me write a stupid journal for the summer. Of course, getting busted for weed earlier this week didn't put me in Ma's good graces. As punishment she's making me get in that dorky Big Brother/Big Sister program. Good bye summer, hello hell. I can picture my summer getting flushed down the toilet. No more friends; no more parties. This totally bites! Ah! I mean, I got caught with a little bit of weed, not a kilo. I told Mom, "You know that if Dad was here, I wouldn't be in trouble." She always yells back about how Dad was a loser and how I should never want to be like him. Well, how about this for a journal entry. I can't do this forever.

Jun 12, 20xx - Dear Journal,

This whole journal thing's becoming OK. I hope my friends never read this. I met Rick today for the second time. He's in his twenties, which would normally make him cool, but he's all religious and stuff. I can't stand that dogma junk. It makes me sick. I don't want to think about it any more. I'm sneaking out the window, probably aught to hide this journal.

Jun 30, 20xx – Dear Journal,

All I can think about is Rick; the guy from Big Brothers. I want to stop thinking about what he said because it makes me weak and sick to my stomach. I was starting to get to like him. He didn't seem so religious the last few times, and he was blaring rock music in his car as he drove me to the movies. On the way back, though, he started talking about God and all the other stuff. I can hardly think straight. I think I'm going to go read that book he gave me since I'm grounded to the house. He called it a 'bible' or something. I don't remember. Oh well.

July 28, 20xx – Dear Journal,

Rick was taking me downtown yesterday when I saw some of my old friends. They were smoking blunts and drinking in an alley. I wish I would have asked Rick to stop so that I could talk to them about God and how I've changed. Life is great. I can't stop thinking about things and ideas and I love it. Well, I would like to write more, but I have to go to church. Thankfully Mom's coming this time. It's so wonderful. Laters.

Jenny Cook -- Letter to Mom

Type of Mini-lesson: Gear switch: letter

Writers know that speaking directly to a person is more electrifying than speaking about them.

Jenny writes a powerful tribute to her mother in a personal letter form. This direct message eloquently makes Jenny's point that people can change each other's lives.

Activity:
Read the letter aloud.
Ask students what all they know about Jenny's message.
What important detail does Jenny <u>not</u> say? How does the reader know it anyway?

Challenge:
Think about a truth you want to convey. See if you can come up with one person who is a real-life example or personification of that truth. Try writing that person a letter to express this.

132

Dear Mom,

Over the years the time we shared was unimaginable. The long walks and evening talks which sometimes lasted into the morning. It seemed like never ending laughter in our home. Even the time I lost your favorite pair of earrings. You still didn't stop loving me. The cooking lessons you put me through to prepare me for college life. How hard you worked to ensure me money for college. All my extra-curricular activities from volleyball games, to spelling bees you attended. You were there for me when my first love broke my heart. Every Sunday you made sure we went to Church. You instilled discipline and good work ethics in me. You made sure when I got my license to warn everyone but you still let me drive the car even after I hit the trashcan. You always told me everything would be ok. You prepared me to live on my own and taught me how to clean the toilet. You made sure I was taken care of because you knew one day I would be on my own. What you taught me I still apply to my life everyday. I didn't expect you to leave so soon and now I understand why you taught me everything at a young age. Every Sunday I go to Church. It helps me get a little closer to you. You were the person who impacted my life the most in everything I do. Even the simple things make me think of you. I take a walk every evening and think of all the things you taught me. I remember the time you had to buy new trashcans because you let me use the car. You made an impact in my heart like the impact a rock has on the moon. It was you who made me understand life.

> With all my love,
> Your daughter Jennifer

Justin Gallego – Abraham Lincoln

Type of Mini-lesson: Letter and response letter

Writers use letters and response letters to tell stories and to make points.

Justin draws a powerful example from history to make a point about how people can make a difference to the lives of others. He shows this point so clearly, in the voice of a historical character and a response letter from someone.

Activity:

Read the letters.

Notice there's actually a historical error in the response letter. This indicates that the high score reflects this author's writing ability, not historical research.

Challenge:

Look at some sample prompts. Think about historical figures who would be likely voices to speak. Try letters and response letters.

134

Justin Gallego – High school -- O'Connor High School, Northside ISD

Fellow Americans,

     I President Abraham Lincoln, Leader of the Union, hereby ensure the freedom of all men, women, and children (regardless of color) under the Government of the Union. Anyone claiming to own a man as property will be arrested and persecuted. During the duration of these terrible times we must stand together as one whole. For the time of white and black as been abolished! From this era a new Government will arise. A time where we will fight side by side. A time where we will live in peace and harmony as brothers. These desperate times have tried us all. I salute those who have bravely died for our country and bless those people who mourn for them. But as long as there is slavery instated in this land, what we are fighting for will become a meaningless dream. A memory of that one Great land of America, where freedom comes as common as air. Where opportunity was not only for the well and righteous but for all who desire it. For that dream I plead with you join with me and remove our bad deed. Let us abolish slavery once and for all. As a great man spoke these powerful words so shall I united we stand apart we fall.

                        Sincerely,
                        A Lincoln

Mr. President,

     Dear kind sir. I would like to tell you how grateful I am for you putting a stop to slavery. I can now live a fulfilled life get married, watch my children grow just as any other man. I have established my family and am fighting under General Lee. We have never lost a battle and fight with a position of true cause. Every single regiment knows that they are fighting for a true cause. You can see the courage they get after winning a battle. There enthusiasm carries them further than any other army in the world. We believe in you, Thank you.

                    Commander Ronnie James

Adrian Gonzales --Pallbearer

Type of Mini-lesson: Transitions

Transitions drive the piece the same way that a steering wheel drives the direction that a car goes. They can also help in moving a thought from general truism to specific moment.

Adrian uses powerful sentence structure that leads a reader to follow his train of thought. He masterfully moves from a general thought to a specific moment.

Activity:

Get a key word from a prompt, like the word "friendship" in "write about the importance of friendship," and use that key word as the first word in this exercise.)

Write this:

(key word from the prompt, like "friendship") is (now finish this sentence.)

It can be _____ or it can be _____.

What we don't realize is _____.

Regardless of what we think about it, _____.

That's exactly what I saw when _____.

(Does that lead you to a memory?)

Share paragraphs. This was modeled from the opening of Adrian Gonzales's paper. Reread this paper.

Challenge:

See if you can use a pattern like this to move from a truism to a moment.

136

Adrian Gonzales – High school -- Lee High School, North East ISD

Choices are selections we make everyday. They can be choosing what to wear in the morning, what to eat, what music to listen to, or even choosing to pay attention inn class. What we don't realize though is that the smallest of choices can affect our whole future. The choices we make in school, at home, and in society can determine what kind of person we become in life and in society. Regardless of what we think about them, our choices can and will affect us for the rest of our lives. Just as my choice to be a pallbearer at my grandmother's funeral affected me and my life.

When I was ten, my grandmother died on New Year's Day. The fire crackers and parties were silenced for my family. Only tears and grieving were heard from my home. My family was in a state of devastation, but there still were arrangements to be made and people to be called for the funeral.

I was also in a state of shock and confusion along with my own desolation. I was old enough to apprehend it, yet I was too young to embrace it and understand why. I felt lost and empty inside as if my heart had been seized from its place.

When it came closer to the funeral, my mother approached me with both tears and emptiness in her eyes. She asked me if I would be willing to be a pall bearer at her funeral. I didn't know how to respond. I felt empty inside and as if my feet were made of lead. I didn't know if I was strong enough to accept the fact that I would be the one to put my grandmother in her final resting place. Then I thought to myself, "What would she want me to do?" I searched deep inside myself and found my strength and an answer. I told my mom that I would do it.

Now that I look back on my choice, I realize how much it meant to not only me, but my family and my grandmother. I think it gave them all strength to see myself, a ten year old boy, carrying his grandmother's casket to her resting place. It showed them that even though I was in a state of despair. I had made a choice to find the strength inside myself and the choice to carry my grandmother's casket. I think that it also made my grandmother happy and proud to see how strong I was even in the state I was in. It made me stronger and gave me hope for the times I would to through in the future.

Choices don't just determine the food we eat or the clothes that we wear. They determine who we are as a person. They determine both our morals and our future. That's what make choices a true gift.

137

Sarah Hogan -- Divorce Conversation
Type of Mini-lesson: Genre switch: script

Writers often let their points be made by characters in a dramatic form.

Sarah puts her narrative into a script. Her characters speak in dialogue, and scenes are marked by stage directions. She makes this format work perfectly as an alternative to a narrative prose form.

Activity:
Read the script aloud.
How would this piece be different if it were told in regular narrative prose form?

Challenge:
Think about a narrative you've worked on. Could you retell this story in script form?

It's the second day of school and I'm beginning to meet new people. I'm in my third period math and I notice a girl behind me crying.

Anna (me): Hi. I noticed you're crying and look rather lonely. Is there something I can help you with? What's your name?

Megan: My name is Megan and I am just going through a hard time with my parents. They've been married for sixteen years and have recently got a divorce.

Anna: I know who you feel since my parents divorced a while back. It's been hard telling people how I'm living two different lives, since my parents won't stop arguing. So I realize how hard it is for you.

Megan: Yes, my dad has just moved into his new apartment not far away from my mom. It makes me wonder if they ever thought how it would affect my life.

Anna: Before my parents split, they both told me that they still loved me, but they didn't love each other any more. They never could agree on anything.

Megan: That sounds bad. But how do you feel about writing that your parents are divorced on school records and telling your friends two different numbers which house you're at every weekend.

Anna: Yes at first it was miserable and I always tried to get them back together, but I got over it. All the arguing and fighting taught me a lesson -- never marry someone I won't always love.

(Five minutes left of class)

Anna: Well, there is not much time left in class, but what do you have next period?

Megan: Lunch

Anna: Hey, so do I! Do you want to sit with me at lunch?

Megan: Sure.

(Bell rings to let third period out.)

Megan: It's nice to know that I'm not the only person whose parents are divorced. I hate dealing with all the problems they dumped on me, now I have someone to talk to about it.

Lauren Jacobs -- Mike the Punk

Type of Mini-lesson: Recognizable voice

Writers create narrators with their own personalities, styles, voices, and theme songs. Sometimes a narrator's way of speaking reminds you of a personality you recognize, someone you already know.

Lauren's narrator reminds us of the TV show Dragnet, with its theme song striking up in a perfectly recognizable spot.

Activity:
Read this piece aloud, sounding as much like Joe Friday as possible. Pause more than normal at the periods.
After "My name is Brian," sing the "Dun-da-dun-dun" theme song.

Challenge:
Think up other voices that trigger theme songs, like "Black gold. Texas tea."

Try writing in a theme-song-triggering voice and see if a reader "gets it."

140

Mike was a tough kid. The kind that flip you over during lunch and steal your lunch money. A punk. His dad was a drunk, and his mother suffered from extreme paranoia. You can see his home life wasn't exactly making things better. This is where I came in. My name is Brian. I got pulled into the mess of his life by my mother. "Community Service is a fulfilling pastimes" she always says. Yeah right. I just love picking up trash from highways and intersections. I guess this is how I met Mike. The thing with community service is that you work without a lot of scummy, troublesome people, (a.k.a. Mike) He was the baddest of the bad. His school counselor said either that, or short term prison time. His was the obvious choice. Okay, let's talk more about Mike – shall we? He's a bad apple, brown hair, blue eyes, and tall. I wish I was tall. All the guys want to be him, and all the girls want to be with him not me though. I'm just Brian. The regular kid with regular height and regular features. I'm not new, or exciting. Mike is though. He moved here from Detroit, and our small town isn't used to people like him.

So, anyways, back to the story. I met Mike on the intersection of I21 and Mortimer. I remember it so vividly. There was a fight, Mike vs. Jack. The favor was with Jack, but nobody showed it.

"C'mon Mike!" yelled all of the Outcasts and Volunteers. All I could do was watch from the sidelines. Unfortunately, I'm friends with Jack, which is how I got myself into this mess. I jumped in between them before they had a chance to start the actual fighting.

"Stop it now!" I yelled. Jack shoved me aside.

"This is none of your business. It's between me and him." Jack made a gesture toward Mike. You could see the fire in his eyes. Jack had originally been the bad boy of Pleasantville, but since Mike has showed up, Jack's been watching his back, and planning for this one specific moment to tike with an evasive maneuver. It seems the time has come.

"No. I am not backing down." I held my ground.

"Don't make me bring you into this!" He threatened, and turned to me, the fire still burning in those baby blues.

"I said no. I'm not going to risk either of you getting arrested." This is all Jack needed to turn his efforts away from Mike, and on to me.

"Maybe I should kick your ass, Punk?" He stepped closer to me. His large body of 6'1" compared to mine of 5'7" was impressive, if not intimidating. Mike grabbed him and held him back. Why? Jack didn't like this. He tore free. By now, our supervisor had seen it, and came rushing over. When everything was under control, I told her the story, and I didn't lie.

Later on I talked to Mike.

"That was really brave, y' know, what you did, stepping in between us like that. It took guts. I don't really know what compelled me to grab him like that. Maybe it was not backing down."

Then it hit me. Mike, the bully I feared, wasn't all about being a mean person. He had feelings, too. It was as thought something had been sparked between us, and it felt good to have a new friend.

Now we look out for one another. He teaches me things, like mechanics, and I help him with grades. I help him work with his temper and he even has a girlfriend, as well as a whole new attitude towards life.

141

Elisa Leal --O Squatting One

Type of Mini-lesson: Transitions

Writers use transitions to "drive" the direction of a thought.

Elisa's last paragraph is a stunning example of sentence-to-sentence progression, using transition words. Have students do the exercise and then show them Elisa's piece.

Activity:

1. Look at your writing and find (or write) a short sentence that describes someone, like "_____ was_____."

2. Now write a sentence about that person, naming one characteristic of that person. For instance, "My grandmother was kind." Or "My brother was stingy." Now write your sentence and stop. Look up when you are done.

3. Still writing about the same subject, think about one thing that person did that demonstrates that characteristic. In other words, write one thing you saw them do that tells you they are really as you described them.

4. Begin the next sentence with "When asked why he (or she) behaved in this manner," and finish the sentence.

5. Begin the next sentence with "Gradually."

6. Begin the last sentence with "To this day."

7. Share.

Challenge:

Try using this pattern (and similar patterns) when you describe a person.

142

Once, in a bog not far from here, there lived a toad. Timothy Toad, they called him, and he was a very nice toad, though not very pretty. His skin was all brown and warty, and his eyes were yellow and watery. However, despite his appearance, Timothy had many friends.

One day as he was hopping along merrily, Timothy saw a sight that bewitched him. He had laid eyes on a fairy. Not just any fairy, but the Great Fairy of the Bog, other wise known as Magenta. Timothy instantly fell in love with the Great Fairy. He admired her pearly, glossy wings and lusted after the deep violet hue that radiated from the pixies fair skin. Her chestnut hair and light blue eyes beckoned to Timothy and forgetting who and what he was, he stepped forth into the clearing.

Magenta, a beautiful yet narcissistic sprite, took one look at Timothy and nearly flew away. "What business have you here, toad?" Magenta asked naughtily.

"None, except my wish to look upon your grace, for I believe that I am in love," answered Timothy courteously.

"Love? Thou believest that one as lovely as I would take interest in thee? Ha! Surely you jest, O Squatting One," Magenta replied most disrespectfully. She took notice of the many warts that plagued his brown patchy skin. She became repulsed at the sight of those watery, yellow eyes that looked in admiration at her. "Oh, what funny legs!" She thought to herself, "Surely, I, Magenta, the Great Fairy of the Bog deserve better than this beast?"

"Be gone!" she said finally, after a long pause of silence. "I have no time to sit here and waste my time with one so unworthy as you." And with a flick of glittery wings, she left the poor toad weeping in the clearing.

Timothy was heartbroken. He wouldn't eat and wouldn't sleep. He stopped conversing with friends and neighbors and became bitter towards all. When asked why he behaved in this manner, he merely replied, "Blame it on the so called Great Fairy." Gradually, his friends gave up and just left him alone. To this day, he sits alone on his stump and both curses and longs for the Great Fairy, Magenta.

Cassie Liesman --Father-Daughter Talk
Type of Mini-lesson: Layering thinking

Writers use craft to allow a reader to "slip into the skin of a narrator" and see through their eyes. One of those techniques is weaving mental reactions into dialogue.

Cassie puts her father's words into dialogue, in direct quotes. After the speech, she follows it with what that speech made her think.

Activity:

Highlight the words her father said, using one color.
Highlight her mental reactions, or thoughts, using a different color.

Challenge:
Try writing some dialogue into your piece. After the other person's words, write some mental reactions of the narrator.

144

Cassie K. Liesman – High school -- Lee High School, North East ISD

"Cassie, we need to talk," said my father in a low and suspicious voice. The tone revealed something important, somehow, I knew we were starting a long, monumental discussion.

"Ok, what about," I replied tentatively.

"About, about wills," he stumbled. "I feel now is a good time for you to decide. You are mature enough, and strong enough to make this decision." I think he was more stressed than I was, and he was not even making the choice. "First," he said as he cleared his throat, "we have to talk about Lindsey."

"Um, what do we have to say, we already know she is going to live with you," I announced.

"Yes, but that is what these wills are about, to understand and make clear exactly what happens to her after I'm gone," he said, fading out in the last few words.

"Well, don't plan on dying soon, and maybe by then, who knows, maybe she can support herself."

"Cassie, think of who you are talking about. It's Lindsey. I've told you she will never grow out of her ADD, an extreme learning disability, and even if she could live with it, her social skills just don't function like the rest of the world. She functions on a 5th grade level. She's a ten year old, stuck in a twenty year old body." Wow. It really hit me then, my sister, my lovely twenty-year-old sister will probably never function as a "normal" human being. Someone will always have to at least check up on her or permanently live with her. I took a moment then strongly looked into my father's deep blue eyes. I could see his struggle and fear. Lindsey was his little baby girl and he couldn't and wouldn't let anything happen to her.

"What are my options?" I forcefully asked.

"Great!" he gave a sigh of relief. "There's the possibility of her living with you, putting her in a group home, or finding a foster care situation," he exclaimed, putting a huge emphasis on "living with you." "Now you don't have to decide now, take your time and think it through." I didn't have a clue. I could go all different directions and had so many reasons, but I still ended up with her living with me. It was just the best situation for her, so there was no way around it.

"I want her to live with me." The words just popped out of my mouth. I was confident, but a little startled.

"What? You have decided already? You should take more time," he said, stunned that I replied so quickly.

"No, no, I've decided and I choose to take full responsibility of Lindsey after you are gone."

"You're sure? There's no turning back," he said. "Then sign here and I'll take care of the rest of it. Thank you sweety, you made the right choice."

"Thank you, Daddy," I beamed as I gave him a huge hug.

That night, as I was lying in bed, I realized how an important choice such as signing a will can impact someone's life. For Lindsey, her life will continue, happy as expected, but another choice might not conclude that way. So you have to stop and ask yourself, "How does my choice affect and possibly change someone's life?"

145

Travis Moncus – Hospital Scene
Type of Mini-lesson: Fiction: dead giveaway

Some writers like to leave a reader wondering, and sometimes writers give readers clues . But every once in a while a writer will throw in a dead giveaway.

Travis's story seems completely possible until you reach the very last sentence. Then the reader knows, beyond a shadow of a doubt, that it's at least partly fiction.

Activity:
1. Read the paper.
2. Decide as you go whether this could have happened.
3. Use highlighters to show what you think: green = could <u>not</u> have happened, yellow = could have happened.
4. Compare highlights and discuss.

Challenge:
Try thinking up some other "dead giveaway" clues that a piece might be fiction.

146

Gah, my head is pounding, my heart is racing like it's in the eight-mile relay. My throbbing eyes begging to be ajar, but too heavy for my face to please them. The inside of my nose has this awkward feeling like something's in it, and I can't smell a thing. I'm trying to talk but I can't hear my confused words. I try to raise my pitiful voice but still nothing. "Hellooo?!?" I try to scream. Nothing. My rear end is freezing, it's almost like I'm naked, and I'm laying on tight leather like a couch, but too stern for that. I open my mouth real wide and my left eardrum pops like I'm twenty thousand feet up and we are going through turbulence. Wow, I'm thinking I can hear an air conditioner and a few beeps like a monitor or something along that line. Then the security of my mother's voice made its path through my left ear, "Travis, honey please stay still, please sweetie, we are here. Try not to move, you'll only make it worse."

"Make what worse, Mommy?" She couldn't hear me. Then a cold bee sting like shot dug into my frail right tender thigh…

I woke up to a cold silk hand on my cheek after what seemed like an eternity. I was still confused like in a dazed sense. Two warm lips kissed my cold aching forehead. "Momma?" I mumbled. My left eye seemed to work its way open, and there she was, just like I remembered her. "Yes Trav, it's me."

"Where am I? What is all this?" My right eye was still closed, and I couldn't figure out why it wouldn't open. I couldn't feel my toes tingle or my little fingers wiggle. My whole body felt numb, like it had fallen asleep. I lifted my dense head up off of what I know now is a cold emergency room bed. "Trav, you and Dad were in an accident," my mom tried to explain.

"What!" I screamed. I still couldn't move my body. "Where is he?! Momma, where is he?!

"Travis," an older, unshaven man interrupted, "Travis your father is gone."

"No! No! I don't believe you! My dad will never die!"

"I'm so sorry Travis," he tried to say.

"What happened?! Why am I here?! How?! Why…" I started to cry, still on my back, still numb and still.

"A drunk driver, Travis, a man left the bar last night way past three sheets to the wind, ran a red light and left you paralyzed, your father D.O.A., dead on arrival, and killed himself from the blow," Dr. Marks explained.

"No, you're wrong," I tried to move but couldn't, "I'm not…am I?" I tried my hardest to lift my arms and sit up. Nothing. "Mom, I remember now leaving the ranch last night. Dad wanted to surprise you for your birthday today. Why didn't we just leave today? If I just would've taken a little longer to open and close the gates, Pappa would still be here. Momma he'd still be here."

"Travis, your father is in heaven. He's all better." Mom teared up.

"It's not your fault Travis, the drunk man, son, it's his fault." Forty long years have gone by, and I'm still in this wheel chair, Momma's gone, and I'll never forget the way a drunk changed my life forever.

147

Sherilynn Moore -- Katelyn's Prayer
Type of Mini-lesson: Genre switch: weaving text

Writers often embed one kind of text into another, or shift back and forth between two kinds of text for effect.

Sherilynn weaves together two separate kinds of text, creating a chilling effect. She does this to make a point about how a person can make a difference in the life of another, without ever saying it.

Activity:
Read this piece aloud, using two voices.

Talk about how the woven text worked together.

Challenge:
Think about a piece of writing. Think about what it's about. See if you can come up with some well-known, recognizable text to use with it, the way Sherilynn did. (It could be lyrics to a religious, patriotic, or popular song.)

For more information on weaving text, see Chapter 3 of *Reviving the Essay*, by Gretchen Bernabei.

148

"Our Father who art in heaven, hallowed be thy name…"

About a year and a half ago my mother and father got involved in drugs and alcohol.

"Thy kingdom come, thy will be done on earth as it is in heaven…"

My mother helplessly lies on the couch watching and hypnotized by the TV after taking in too much crack or weed. My dad … well he is a drunkie!!

"Give us this day our daily bread, and forgive our trespasses, as we forgive those who trespass against us…"

On weekdays I have to get what I need myself, because my parents are completely oblivious to the fact that I was ever born.

"And lead us not into temptation, but deliver us from evil . . ."

I remember when I was younger that my mom would take me to the park and we would have a picnic. She would make elegant and elaborate meals – not just peanut butter and jelly sandwiches.

"For thy is the kingdom and the power, and glory forever…"

My name is Katelyn Rashea Dickerson, I'm 11 years old and live in a one bedroom apartment. As I told you previously, my mom does drugs and my dad drinks to his hearts content. My father goes out every night and doesn't come home till 2 maybe 3 in the morning. When he does … he is like a bull in a china closet, throwing things and slamming doors and yelling at everything. One night he busted into my room and pulled me to the living room, ran his finger along the entertainment center and said, "Do you see this dust; even though I had not seen anything. I had dusted it earlier that day. "Y-y-yes sir I stuttered." "I want it spotless when I get back in here!" he exclaimed. And of course he isn't gone long enough for me to finish, Oh NO!! he hits me till I can barely stand … then it is off to the bathroom. He bangs my head against the mirror and the counter top after a few grueling minutes of punishment, it is over, he has had his fun for the night. One night he came home in a drunk rage and beat the hell out of me. He stomped off and got a gun. Two shots, one for him and the other for my mom.

Ever since my father turned into a monster I had been afraid of anyone who tries to touch me – even if they are trying to help.

…Amen"

Writers use many rhetorical devices in their writing.

Keri masterfully breaks out lists with her sentences, painting clear images. In this way, she elegantly says a lot in a short space.

Activity:
1.   Look at the sentence: "She washed my uniform nightly, took me to all my classes, coached me when I fought, helped me practice at home and always reminded me to brush my teeth before class."

That sentence's power lies in the list of specifics. We could rewrite it to be much less powerful like this: "She did so many things."

2. Look at the last sentence. How would you rewrite it to be less powerful?

Challenge:
Try taking one of your own sentences and see if you can break out a list in the sentence.

150

"Yeah, but she's a nerd."

As a young girl I wasn't your popular, athletic, brunette goddess. I was the blonde-haired girl who always got straight "A"s and made friends with all the teachers. I wore my school uniform and couldn't shoot a basketball into the hoop even if my life depended on it. When I finally did find a sport that captured my interest, there wasn't a team for my age group that I could join. Therefore, my mom enrolled me in a month's worth of Tae Kwon Do classes.

I instantly fell in love with the sport. My addiction to doing better drove me to become a member of the Jr. Olympic team. I medaled at all my tournaments; I'm the most proud of getting second place at Nationals for Jr. Olympics. Many people questioned why I never gave up. By taking a look at my planner you could tell how devoted I was: five or six days a week I was at the studio practicing.

My alarm sounded off, "Beep. Beep. Beep," and I rolled over, very sore from the previous day's work out. "5:30 a.m., right on time," I would say every Sunday morning as I pressed the snooze button. When I finally forced myself out of bed, I got dressed and went to practice. "There are three thirds to winning: you, your coach, and your support team. If you're missing any of those, there is absolutely no way you can walk or limp out of a ring with a gold medal around your neck," Coach Levell said to us every weekend.

After 8th grade we moved from California to Texas. I had to start from ground zero. Everything was new and I had no friends. I started Tae Kwon Do at a new studio. This was supposed to be the year I tested for my black belt, a goal I had had for four years. However, I wasn't nearly as motivated or dedicated. I skipped practices, my endurance slowly began to weaken and I became more active in other things.

But encouragement isn't only about physically rooting someone on; it's also about knowing someone deep down and helping them in any way so that they get to where they need to be. My lack of enthusiasm did not go unnoticed; my mom was right there. My mom was my savior, my provider, my best friend and my number one cheerleader. She knew how badly I've always wanted my black belt and she encouraged me to get it. She washed my uniform nightly, took me to all my classes, coached me when I fought, helped me practice at home and always reminded me to brush my teeth before class. When there was no one left for me to turn to, my mom was already standing there and helping me get back up and kicking again.

When the test finally came and I waited to be called up to perform, I got nervous. I had sweaty palms, a panicking quickness in my breath and I only heard, "Stop now, you can't do it," thundering to the pulsating roar in my head. The only thing that kept my focus was knowing that someone who believed in me was back there cheering and mentally chanting, "Impossible and can't are not words in our dictionary." After seven hours had passed, I walked out of the studio as a black belt. I had "passed with flying colors." But people don't win in Tae Kwon Do out of sheer luck, the gold medalists are the ones with the most skill and the best support team.

In my life my mom played many roles, but none compare to her role as my #1 cheerleader. Encouragement from others is like a crutch from the heart to aid someone in desperation. Because of my crutch, I'm a black belt, a junior Olympian, a straight "A" student, and a very thankful human.

151

Kendall Soler -- Dear Coach

Type of Mini-lesson: Genre switch: story of a letter

Writers sometimes embed various pieces of writing (or primary sources) into other writing. This gives a reader a refreshing change in the reading.

Kendall creates a situation and a letter that results, moving the reader into her own composing (and revising) process. We, the readers, are treated to the whole gritty context of the letter which makes it juicy for us!

Activity:
Read the piece and draw a highlight border around the letter(s) in the piece. See how the piece would be different with a description of the letter instead.

Challenge:
Think about embedding a letter or note or e-mail into a piece of writing.

152

Please Consider This

The streetlights seemed to flash by as fast as lightning. Never had I found myself so wound up and infuriated by a single individual. My mother and I vented and bashed my club volleyball coach the whole thirty minutes home from the Austin Convention Center after losing the finals to get first in the entire tournament.

"She told Shelby that she wasn't a good volleyball player and she needed to be replaced," I explained as I rolled my eyes at the thought of my best friend on the team being kicked off. "It's impossible for coach to do that."

"I wish that woman would be able to see what she looks like screaming and throwing a fit from the sidelines," my mom let out a heavy chuckle.

We both agreed something had to be done about this. I was exhausted from the constant drama that was brought with this new coach of ours. Talking face to face with coach about her own mistakes was something that everyone knew not to do.

I'll write her a letter, I thought to myself and a smile came to my face from ear to ear, very content with my idea.

Dear Coach, You disgust me…

Hah, I thought. This needs to be encouraging and not make her feel horrible about herself. I began again…

Dear Coach,

Throughout the season so far, the relationship between your players (including myself) and you has gotten worse and worse. I feel like I need to bring to attention that everyone on the team is terrified of getting on the court and playing in front of you because you have put too much pressure on us. Instead of using punishment for discipline and scare tactics, I think it might be better to use goals and achievements as a way of getting us all to get fired up to play.

Another issue is the fact that all of us players have played together for 2 years now and never have we had any drama or bad situations on the team. Now this year, it seems like our team is being split apart and this is because of the comments that you have made to us individually about what another player says. I think it would be a good idea if you would keep what you have heard to yourself because clearly the method that you are using is not working out too well.

In the long run however, you are an amazing coach and really know the game. I, myself, and my teammates have improved and learned so much. Thank you for that. Please consider this information.

Your player,
#24 Kendall Soler

I set my pen down and took a deep breath. I hope this works, I thought to myself.

Amy Zhang – I Am China
Type of Mini-lesson: Anaphora

Writers use patterns with their words, patterns of all kinds.

Amy writes "I grew up in China." She follows with a compelling anaphora in the second paragraph, to give the reader plenty of glimpses into her sentence.

Activity:
Imitate this pattern and see if it words for you.
Write this sentence:
I grew up …(tell where).

Finish each of these sentences with something to do with the place you mention.
  I first spoke…
  I first learned to walk…
  I first touched…
  I first made friends…
  I first learned…

Now re-read Amy's second paragraph and listen to her pattern again.

Challenge:
 Try including a pattern like Amy's next time you need to elaborate on a simple sentence.

Online resource: www.virtualsalt.com/rhetoric.htm

154

My friends have always said that I was too sensitive to words like "China" and "Asian", that I may not hear them when they call "Amy" yet I will turn around alarmingly whenever anyone mentions "Chinese". I cannot deny it. China is a place that I will feel a strong connection to till the end of my days. I guess it's just when you are living in a foreign country. When you are surrounded by all these people who look and speak a different language from you, when you are the minority that you feel the perpetual isolation, that you come to cherish all of the memories you've had in your motherland, which in my case, is China.

I grew up in China. I spoke my first word "mama" in Chinese, while holding out my hand to grab the piece of sesame chicken in her hands. I first learned how to walk in a Chinese apartment, small and crowded, yet full of adventure to the toddler me. I first touched the enigmatic wonder of literature in Chinese, painfully reciting the lines of poet Li Po before my teacher in a schoolhouse filled with the smell of green tea. I first made my friends in China, as I successfully entered the best middle school in my city after I studied a whole year for the entrance exam. I first learned my morals of life in China as my parents punished me severely for lying. I realized that I was a free-willed person who strives for best all the time.

I am like a migrating bird, taking all of the memories from China. My homeland, flying through the clouds to America, mixing the mud and water, and building my home here. My life made me connected to my country, which will never diminish. I am China.

155

L.G. – Elaine

Type of Mini-lesson: Strong Feelings

We have feelings and thoughts all the time, sometimes mild and sometimes so strong they're almost out of control. Writers put these changing thoughts and emotions into words, which allows a reader to see the whole process.

L.G. weaves her thoughts and feelings together as they grow stronger, giving readers a clear and rare glimpse inside someone's head just as they flash with fury.

Activity:
Write one-sentence answers to these questions:
1: What was one feeling you have felt <u>very</u> strongly?
2. At that time, what did you believe caused the feeling?
3. What do you now believe caused the feeling?

Now look at this excerpt from L.G.'s paper:

After this, I was more raged than I had ever been in my life, and I thought it was at Elaine, but now I realize that it was at myself, because she was right.

Challenge:
See if you can add thoughts/feelings patterns similar to this in your writing.

156

I was always a joyous child, that is, until I reached my second year of Junior High School, and my dearest cousin, Jessica, who was more of an older sister figure to me, was killed in a terrible car wreck. It was all dreamlike and I was sure I would wake up and that none of it would be real, but it didn't go away. Jessica had been the one person I could talk to that I could tell anything, and now that freedom was gone. She was gone, and I was so mad. I was mad at her for leaving me here alone, at God for taking her away, and at the world. I was mad at myself for not being able to change it. I lived that year of my life like I was stuck in a black hole, full of depression and anger, and no matter what anyone said I refused to come back out into the sunshine. I was stubborn and obnoxious, and for some reason I felt it was my right, because the world had treated me poorly. Nobody stopped me either, because I guess they would feel guilty after what I had been through. Nobody that is, until I met my match, Elaine, the new girl, who was exactly the opposite of myself at that point in my life. She was cheery and full of sunshine, and I hated her. One day at lunchtime in the cafeteria, when I was sitting by myself in the back corner table of the cafeteria as usual, she came and plopped down right next to me. "Hi, I'm Elaine," she said exuberantly as she held out a small hand with pretty rings and pink polished nails. I looked up at her momentarily and then continue eating. "Well, aren't you going to introduce yourself?" she said obnoxiously. "No," I replied stubbornly. "Well, that's kind of rude. So why do you always sit here in the back by yourself? You can join me and my friends. They're very accepting. I just moved here last week." I retorted, "Just leave me along. I sit alone because I am alone. We all are." She looked shocked and hurt as she replied, "What makes you say that?" "Look, the one person I knew I could count on to always be there is dead. Just get out of my face. I don't need your sympathy or anyone's." Her smile dropped instantly and she glared at me before stomping off saying, "Look, I'm not stupid. You think you're the only one with problems, and that because of them you can treat people however you want. How much more self-centered can you get? My mother died from breast cancer, but you don't see me sitting all alone in a corner feeling sorry for myself." After this, I was more raged than I had ever been in my life, and I thought it was at Elaine, but now I realize that it was at myself, because she was right. I went home still storming mad, crawled into bed and cried myself to sleep even though it was still only the afternoon. When I woke up, I had cooled off a lot, and I just lay there and for some reason I knew that I had to change. I couldn't keep this up, it was too painful and tiresome. It was like seeing the light at the end of a seemingly interminable dark tunnel and like a breath of fresh air after a deep plunge all at once. The next day, when I returned to school I approached Elaine, and apologized for my harsh words, and she of course being a most pure-hearted person accepted and offered me a new chance. I went from being lonely to having a life full of friends where I let my family back in, and I owe it all the loving heart and courage of a girl who is now my best friend. Never again would I spend too much time feeling sorry for myself, instead of living my life.

25 Things You Can Do With Your Best Student Samples With 10 Minutes a Day

So you've collected a great group of score point 4 papers from last year's test.

In the old days, we used to just read them and say "Ahh. " Those days are gone. Now, they're incredible teaching tools, far better than anything from outside sources..

What might you do with them in class? First, get signatures from students and their parents, granting you permission to publish the papers with the students' names on them.

****

1. Read one aloud and see what you notice.
2. Do "Say back" as a large-group. Instructions are in <u>Acts of Teaching</u> by Joyce Armstrong Carroll.
3. Find one with great linking and convert it to a template for imitation.
4. Devolve one. For examples, go to www.trailofbreadcrumbs.net.
5. Read openings and listen to the variety.
6. List genres of samples you find.
7. Make a chart of strong verbs.
8. Make posters of your school's best papers, and line up that great work in a "hall of fame" display. (You'll need permission from the authors and their parents, to post the student names.)
9. Get a "How I did it" commentary from writers, and post annotations with the essay.
10. Look at interesting punctuation across several papers.
11. Find essays with very different voices, and read several aloud. Ask students to describe the differences in voices.
12. Type up one without any punctuation, and try to read it aloud. Compare it to its original.
13. Take a look at dialogue across several papers.
14. Do a highlighter hunt for brushstrokes (For more information, see Harry Noden's *Image Grammar*. Or visit http://www.heinemann.com/shared/onlineresources/0466/demo03.html).
15. Draw what you hear.

158

16. Underline every other sentence, and read with two voices. Listen for variety in sentence lengths.
17. Do a vocal color-coding: listen to the first 4 words in every sentence, in alternating voices.
18. Make a labyrinth on the floor, with corners holding examples of whatever you find in the gorgeous essays, like extraordinary vocabulary, striking verbs, rhetorical devices. Then use it as a "walk" for students writing their own essays.
19. Devolve one sentence from specific to general.
20. Read one aloud, and write letters to the author.
21. Do a highlighter-hunt for truisms or life lessons.
22. Do a highlighter-hunt for ba-da-bing sentences.
23. Draw a "3D Memory" target. For more information, see Linda Stubbs' lesson at www.trailofbreadcrumbs.net.
24. Draw, or map out, the text structure.
25. Search for words from the prompt, to see where or if they appear in the piece.

Questions and Answers

Why are there more 7th grade papers than the other levels?

We don't know why, but there were more papers submitted from seventh grade than any other level. We published all the verifiable, permissioned pieces we received.

What would these papers actually receive on the actual test?

They all received a score point of 4 in Texas, during the TAKS test years. So they would all receive a 4. They actually did.

But some of them don't start with the prompt.

We noticed that.

Some of them don't even mention the prompt.

We noticed that too. You could probably read a piece and list some prompts that might have sparked that piece.

Students at my school don't have skills like these.

All the more reason to work from really effective models.

We don't teach the kinds of kids who score 4s.

There aren't kinds of kids. There are kinds of papers. Over and over, we've seen students who repeatedly score 1s suddenly, with some clear instruction, score a 3 or 4.

Wouldn't it be better to spend our time working on grammar and sentence structure first, and then eventually work our way into paragraphs and longer compositions?

No. Time is a precious commodity in school, and we won't ever be given more of it. Google up the research report called "Writing First" and read what it has to say about teaching grammar out of context. It cites studies which show students actually *lose ground* in writing skills when teachers take time out to do grammar units.

Why hasn't TEA told us these things?

They have, over and over. They've published rubrics and scoring training tapes, and they keep showing up at conferences asking for more compositional risks, more authentic writing, more diversity in approaches, more real writing skills.

Why aren't there any papers from my school?

Send us some. We'll most likely be doing an update with more papers in the near future. Make sure and download the permission-to-publish form and send that with the test paper. If you'd like to submit pieces, you can find everything you need at www.trailofbreadcrumbs.net.

161

NOTES

NOTES

NOTES

NOTES

NOTES

NOTES

NOTES